VEGAN
LOW-CARB
COOKBOOK

Quick and Easy Budget Meals

JORDAN RILEY

YOUR FRIENDLY GUIDE

Disclaimer from Jordan:

I did not write this cookbook for the benefit of expert cooks or committed vegans.

I wrote this book for beginners and curious non-vegans like you.

This book is for those who know little about veganism and are harried and pressed for time. You don't have all the time, energy, and resources to make elaborate meals for yourself and your loved ones.

Come and join me. I want less judgment about your/our food choices and more encouragement and kindness.

Please do your own due diligence with respect to any physical or mental health claims from health or food bloggers or cookbooks.

- Dietary changes (such as a change to the vegan diet) impact the human body and may not be suitable for certain ages.

- It is of vital importance to ensure that you are getting enough nutrition.

- Please take care not to skew your online search results by using biased keywords such as "health benefits of...". Such searches may not yield information on any negative health effects, which may be important.

- For best search results, you can use neutral keywords like "veganism and health" in popular online search engines to get the full picture on this very important topic. You and your near and dear ones will be glad you did.

"Veganism is just another path among many valid ones;

Home-Cooking is just *another* vehicle among many good ones;

Total health—mental, physical, emotional, and spiritual—is *the* destination."

– Jordan Riley

Book Design by: **Ravi Ramgati**

Table of Contents

CHAPTER 1

Introduction To
Low-Carb Vegan Diet

L ow-carb vegan diets are becoming increasingly popular. Many find that this type of diet can help with weight loss and provide other health benefits. Traditionally, low-carb diets have relied heavily on meats, but there are plenty of plant-based options. A low-carb diet involves eating meals that contain few carbohydrates and plenty of healthful fats. The diet emphasizes the importance of fats and protein.

Vegetarian and vegan people do not eat meat, poultry, fish, or shellfish. Vegetarians tend to eat other animal-derived products, including dairy, eggs, and honey, while vegans do not. Vegetarian and vegan diets can be heavy in carbs, from grains, bread, starchy vegetables, and fruits. However, following a low-carb vegetarian or vegan diet is entirely possible.

Vegetarians, pescatarians, and omnivores can all enjoy vegan sources of protein and fat, as well as other low-carb vegan options. Vegetarians can enjoy low-carb vegan options and incorporate dairy and egg products. Pescatarians and omnivores may also benefit from adding low-carb vegan and vegetarian meals to their diets.

There is no clear cutoff for what constitutes a low-carb diet. The amount of carbs a person can eat varies from plan to plan. It is important for each person to find a diet plan that suits their needs and goals. Consider talking to a doctor or dietician before making significant dietary changes. A healthcare professional can take into account an individual's health and advise about the suitability of a low-carb diet. Counting the number of carbs in each meal is an important part of following the diet. Developing meal plans can make this simpler.

What is Veganism?

The term "vegan" was chosen by combining the first and last letters of "vegetarian." It was coined in 1944 by a small group of vegetarians who broke away from the Leicester Vegetarian Society in England to form the Vegan Society. They chose not to consume dairy, eggs, or any other products of animal origin, in addition to refraining from meat, as do vegetarians.

Veganism is a way of living that seeks to exclude, as far as possible and practicable, all forms of exploitation of, and cruelty to, animals for food, clothing, or any other purpose.

It is a type of vegetarian diet that excludes meat, eggs, dairy products, and all other animal-derived ingredients. Many vegans also do not eat foods that are processed using animal products, such as refined white sugar and some wines.

Vegan refers to either a person who follows this way of eating or to the diet itself. That is, the word vegan can be an adjective used to describe a food item, as in, "This curry is vegan," or it can be used as a noun, as in, "Vegans like cookies, too."

What is the Difference Between Veganism and Low-Carb Veganism?

Most people usually wonder if the vegetarian diet and the vegan diet are the same things. They are not the same. All vegans are vegetarians, but all vegetarians are not vegans. This is because while the vegetarian diet advocates for plant-based foods; there are some variations of the diet that allow for some animal-sourced products like dairy, honey, and eggs. This is not the case when it comes to vegans. Vegans only allow plant-based foods into their diet and prohibit the consumption of any animal flesh and animal-related food, including dairy, honey, and eggs.

Some people go for a variation of the vegan meal plan where they eat raw food. This is referred to as the raw vegan diet. Vegans eliminate all animal source products from their food. Their food is rich in vegetables, fruits, and whole grains. A vegan diet is usually low in fat, and it can be challenging to eat enough protein on a daily basis. Most foods in this diet are low-calorie foods.

Vegans are believed to be thinner and healthier compared to omnivores. They are also said to have a lower body mass index (BMI) and also lower cholesterol levels. This is because their food mostly consists of fresh fruits and vegetables. Vegetables and fruits are great sources of vitamins, which are greatly needed by the body. They are also excellent sources of minerals and other nutrients essential for the human body.

Why Do People Choose to Go Vegan?

There are several reasons why a person might choose to go vegan. These reasons are:

- Better health. This is because plant-based diets are said to reduce the risk of certain diseases, apart from offering nutrients needed by the body to promote good health.

- Protect the animals and environment at large. Most vegans are pro-animal life and choose the vegan way to protect the lives of animals. Some vegans don't even have items made from animal products as jewelry, part of their home decor, or anything.

Low-Carb Diet

Since all there is to highlight, the vegan diet has been discussed. What is the low-carb diet?

This diet is known to come in different names; some people refer to it as a ketogenic diet or a low-carb, high-fat diet. This food plan emphasizes rich sources of fat, moderate sources of proteins, and limited consumption of carbs. This particularly goes to mean most starchy vegetables, fruits and grains are largely excluded from this diet. The same cannot be said for the vegan food plan. You have to minimize your carb intake under all costs in this diet but increase your fat intake.

The idea behind most low-carb diets is to force your body into a state of ketosis. Ketosis is a state in which your body uses fat for energy instead of carbohydrates. This diet involves removing carbohydrates from your diet until your body and brain are forced to utilize another form of energy. When you eat less than 50 grams of carbohydrates per day, which is what most people following a keto diet eat every day, your body eventually runs out of fuel, which is commonly known as glucose. This takes about three to four days to happen. After this, your body will start to break down fat for energy. This process of using ketones for energy, for fueling your body, is called ketosis. In simple terms, when you are in ketosis, your body will start breaking down and using its stored fats for energy.

What Do I Need to Get Started with a Low-Carb Vegan Diet?

With our lives turning into a work-from-home schedule, most of us have grown health-conscious. We have started stressing about regular exercises, yoga, and a proper diet to strengthen our bodies and immunity. Some of us have chosen to top it up with a ketogenic or other low-carb diet to lose unwanted weight. These diets make you cut down on your carbohydrate intake and redirect your focus to healthy fats and protein. If you are planning to go on a low-carb diet, here are some things you need to start with.

Want to start a low-carb diet? Take note of these:

1) Make a diet chart.

A low-carb diet doesn't mean shunning carbohydrates completely. So, to balance it well, making a diet chart becomes the most important step before starting a low-carb diet. For example, choose to have fruits and milk for breakfast, in addition to the proteins. For lunch or dinner, you can have whole grain rotis or stir-fry vegetables. It is essential to plan every meal for better results of the diet you are following.

2) Carb refeeding.

This is a popular term among those following keto, paleo, and other diets. It's the process of including carbohydrates in your meals periodically while you are on a diet. Balancing your proteins with a bit of carb once in a while can be beneficial for the body.

3) Cut all the refined carbs.

While you are making room for good carbs, make sure you slowly start eliminating all bad and refined ones from your diet. Sugary cookies, biscuits, cereals, refined pasta, and bread are all high in refined carbs that you must try to cut down as soon as possible. Aerated drinks and soda are also a big no-no.

4) Eat the right food.

Ensure that you remain amply hydrated, and your diet is rich in green leafy vegetables that will help keep your fiber levels high and promote gut health. If you are a non-vegetarian, you can indulge in chicken, eggs, and meat as long as you do not overeat. Also, on a low-carb diet, dairy products like paneer, cheese, butter as well as nuts and seeds are your best friends. But like anything else, moderation is key even when you are snacking.

CHAPTER 2

What Will I Get From The Low-Carb Vegan Diet?

Health Benefits and Sustainability

Having good health free from illnesses is everyone's goal. Good exercise, a healthy lifestyle, and strictly following a nutritious diet will help you achieve this.

Two of the major health trends today are the ketogenic and vegan diets. Though these two might not look like they fit perfectly with each other, since the vegan diet relies mainly on a high amount of carbohydrates as the key source of energy, vegans can still follow a ketogenic lifestyle, thus, helping them achieve the health benefits of both. The vegan keto diet offers a wide array of health benefits.

1. Prevents and Fights Diabetes and Obesity

Based on studies, the ketogenic diet is an effective way of reducing medications in patients with diabetes. Since the keto-vegan diet limits carbohydrate intake and ensures a sugar-free diet, it lowers blood sugar levels, significantly decreasing the risk of developing diabetes in the future. For those who already have diabetes, this diet helps them lower insulin dosages or eliminates medications in as short as a few weeks.

2. Lowers the Risk of Having a Heart Disease

Heart disease is one of the leading causes of death worldwide. It can be triggered by several health conditions but is mainly due to lack of exercise, obesity, and an unhealthy diet.

Most people think that having a high-fat diet is not good for the heart. Recent studies show that an intake of good fats is safe and provides long-term health benefits. A continuous keto-vegan diet does not show any significant increase in cardiac events, but it even lowers the number of triglycerides, fat molecules circulating in your bloodstream that are linked to heart disease.

3. Improves Over-All Mental Health

Studies show that the keto-vegan diet improves mental cognition, making you more focused and improving your critical thinking skills. This lifestyle keeps your brain young and sharp. Having a balanced diet – low-carb, rich in good fats, and moderate in proteins – protects your neurovascular functions, which helps in maintaining good cognitive skills.

The keto-vegan diet offers both protection from and prevention of cancer by minimizing carbohydrates and replacing them with healthy fats. Reduction of the consumption of starchy vegetables and sugary fruits will actively starve cancer cells. A lot of keto-vegan staples help prevent cancer cells from growing.

4. Helps in Improving Vision and Eyesight

Cataracts and glaucoma, progressive diseases that cause poor vision or even blindness, can be prevented through a keto-vegan diet—having a diet that is low in carbs but rich in good fats can help the retinal cells become healthy and also prevents cell degeneration.

Since the keto-vegan diet prevents diabetes, potential connections between it and glaucoma are reduced. Even people who already have glaucoma can improve their vision and slow down, or even stop, the progression of the disease.

5. Stabilizes Hormones

Hormones are chemical messengers in the body. Hormonal imbalances can be chaotic. Ketosis affects your hormones in a good way. Through this, your body lowers the levels of insulin through the elimination of sugar in your diet. Aside from that, levels of leptin, a type of hormone that suppresses hunger, are reduced, which will help you regulate your eating habits.

6. Provides Higher Energy Levels to Help You Get Through the Day

A high intake of carbohydrates can make you feel tired. When you consume food high in carbs (pizza, for example), the starches present in the food are broken down to glucose. In this process, your body requires insulin to move the glucose from the bloodstream. Our bodily functions require this energy. After consuming excess carbohydrates, there will be a spike in energy but will be quickly followed by a big drop making you feel sluggish and tired after the meal.

In a vegan diet, you will experience none of these issues. Your body will now rely on fats instead of carbohydrates. It won't require energy from carbs. Too much insulin production will be prevented because your body can now use stored fat at any time. Through this, you will enjoy a continuous stream of energy throughout the day.

Meal Costs and Budgets

It's tough eating healthy on a budget. Throw in strict fat, carb, and protein ratios, and your grocery list starts to feel like a tug-of-war between macros and money.

Follow these tips to stick with keto without breaking the bank.

1. DIY your snacks

Keto is all the rage these days, which means the snack aisle is chock-full of keto-friendly bars, nut butter, fat bombs, shakes, and protein powders.

Packaged snacks are convenient, but they also cost a pretty penny. So skip the processed foods and grab a handful of nuts instead. DIY = more bang for your buck.

2. Don't forget the veggies

It's easy to think that eating keto = butter, cheese, and meat. But you can and should fill your cart and plate with affordable veggies too!

Do you want to get super thrifty? Rice your own cauliflower. Spiralize your own zoodles. Eat a giant salad where meat shines as an accessory instead of the main event.

3. Bank on black soybeans

Aren't beans too carby for ketosis?

In most cases, yes. But black soybeans are a magical exception. Clocking in at about 1 net carb per 1/2 cup, they're a yummy, cheap, keto-friendly alternative to regular black beans and chickpeas. Fill your plates, friends!

4. Say it with us: Buy in bulk

Buying massive amounts of staples like nuts is an easy way to save time and money. That's especially true when you're stocking up on $$$ items like almonds and cashews.

Pro tip: Keep bulk items fresh by storing them properly. Nuts should be kept in a cool, dry place — usually, a back cabinet or pantry shelf is just fine.

5. Head to the freezer section

Frozen fruits and veggies are often cheaper than their fresh counterparts. And if you're hankering for fruit — a real treat for keto eaters — you'll find a rainbow of raspberries, blueberries, blackberries, and more in the freezer section.

The best part? Frozen foods won't go bad for months. This is especially important for fruit since you'll probably be eating it as only an occasional treat. (Half a cup of blackberries clocks in at about 11.5 grams of carbs.)

Preparation Considerations: Utensils and Equipment

Preparation is key

When you plan your meals, you know exactly what each breakfast, lunch, and dinner costs. You get to control what you spend.

One of the easiest ways to adopt a healthy lifestyle is to start cooking for yourself, but doing so can be challenging for those who don't have the proper kitchen tools. But as a vegan, what tools do you need?

1. Juicer

Vegetable juices can be the most Nutritions: al component to a healthy vegan diet, which is why a device such as an Omega Juice Cube is essential. This compact juicer chews through plant fibers with a convenient storage cavity, providing a way to get your digestive enzymes with an abundance of vitamins and minerals. Plus, the Juice Cube operates at low speeds of 80 RPMs, meaning there's no foaming, no clogging, and no heat build-up. Beyond fruit and vegetables, this multi-purpose kitchen tool can also make nut butter, nut milk, soy milk, and baby food and grind coffee beans and herbs.

2. Chopper and adjustable slicer

Instead of spending hours making sure every cut is equal, tools such as the All-in-1 Vegetable Slicer make it easy and efficient for home cooks to dice vegetables and fruit. The product allows users to create uniform slices thanks to julienne, chop, dice, cut, and grate settings.

The efficiency and usefulness of this product are especially convenient for someone who cooks primarily with vegetables, as this tool allows users to slice fast and safely with easy cleanup.

3. Tofu Press

Made for the vegan foodie, the TofuXpress transforms tofu into a firm texture by removing liquid from the tofu. After the water is removed, simply marinate your tofu to your liking and enjoy! Even better? The TofuXpress can also be used to press vegetables and make vegan cheeses, yogurt cheese, and Greek-style yogurt.

4. Spiralizer

Transform healthy starches, vegetables, and fruit into noodle options in seconds with The Inspiralizer. This easy-to-use gadget has four different noodle shape options (ribbon, fettuccine, linguine, and spaghetti) to achieve your desired texture, consistency, and taste. For recipe inspiration, Inspiralized.com shares recipes organized by vegetables for easy access.

5. Avocado cutter

Avocados are a delicious source of protein in many vegan kitchens. Thankfully, the Flexicado tool is equipped to cut, pit, slice, and scoop the green fruit safely and quickly. Perfect when preparing guacamole, making avocado toast, or when adding avocado to salads, this tool eliminates the need for knives and keeps your hands clean.

6. Food processor

When preparing plant- and wheat-based meals, it's necessary to have a tool that makes chopping vegetables and preparing dough easier. This is where the 11 Cup Performance Dicing Food Processor comes in, as the product is ideal for those who want to take raw almonds and turn them into almond butter or for those lazy folks who don't want to spend their afternoons chopping vegetables.

7. Cookware set

Cookware Set with Stainless Steel Lids allows cooks to steam vegetables and make homemade sauces and crispy tofu with ease. In addition to evenly distributing heat when cooking, these stainless steel lids lock in the moisture when preparing steamed dishes. Furthermore, each piece in this set provides options for preparing an array of foods such as stir-fries, veggie burgers, and grains.

CHAPTER 3

What Are The Other Benefits Of Low Carb-Vegan Diet?

L ow Carb-Vegan Diet are not essential for life, but eating the right kind may benefit your health.

On the Environment

Animal agriculture takes a devastating toll on the earth. It is an inefficient way of producing food since feed for farm animals requires land, water, fertilizer, and other resources that could otherwise have been used directly for producing human food.

Animal agriculture's dependence on higher yields accelerates topsoil erosion on our farmlands, rendering land less productive for crop cultivation and forcing the conversion of wilderness to grazing and farmlands. Animal waste from massive feedlots and factory farms is a leading cause of pollution in our groundwater and rivers.

In a time when population pressures have become an increasing stress on the environment, there are additional arguments for a vegan diet. The United Nations has reported that a vegan diet can feed many more people than an animal-based diet.

On Animal

While vegetarians choose not to eat animals, vegans also avoid eating dairy, eggs, and honey, as well as not wearing fur, leather, wool, down, or using cosmetics or chemical products tested on animals.

Why vegan? Veganism, the natural extension of vegetarianism, is an integral component of a true cruelty-free lifestyle. Living veganism provides numerous benefits to animals' lives, the environment, and our own health through a healthy diet and lifestyle.

As with any mammal, cows produce milk only when pregnant and stop after their calves have been weaned. When a dairy cow delivers a female calf, the calf becomes a dairy cow herself, born to live in the same conditions as her mother. But when a dairy cow delivers a male calf, the calf is sold to a veal farm within days of birth, where he is tethered to a stall, deprived of food and exercise, and soon slaughtered for meat.

Today's farms are not like the ones most of us learned about in school; they are mechanized factories where an animal's welfare is of little concern compared to profit. Veganism emerges as the lifestyle most consistent with the philosophy that animals are not ours to use.

Starting Your Own Sustainable Vegetable or Herb Garden

Vegetable gardening at home can be a way to save money while you get up close and personal with nature. For example, even just one plant can be super affordable (think $3 to $5) and provide up to 10 pounds of tomatoes over the season (which can easily run you $20 or more). Growing tomatoes and other favorite vegetables or herbs from seeds can save you even more money. You'll also find that the flavor and texture of garden-grown produce are even better than what you're used to finding at the grocery store. Dig into these tips and tricks to get your vegetable garden off to a strong start.

1. Start with a Small Space

If you're a beginner gardener, start small. It's better to be thrilled by what you produce in a small garden than to be frustrated by the time commitment a big one requires. It's also best to learn a few gardening basics before investing tons of time and money in this new hobby. You'll get a feeling for how much time gardening takes. You'll find out if you like spending time outside planting, watering, and weeding. You'll learn how much produce you and your family can eat over the course of a summer.

A good size for a beginner's vegetable garden is 6x6 feet. Select up to five types of vegetables to grow, and plant a few of each type. You'll get plenty of fresh produce for your summer meals, and it will be easy to keep up with the chores. Growing vegetables in containers is also a good way to start out.

2. Grow What You Love to Eat

What do you like to eat? Your answer will tell you what you should plant in your vegetable garden. There are also a few other things to keep in mind when deciding what you want to grow.

- **Be Picky About Varieties**

  Pay close attention to the description on the seed packet, tag, or label. Each variety of vegetables comes with certain characteristics. Some produce smaller plants ideal for containers or small gardens. Other varieties offer better disease resistance, improved yields, or better heat- or cold tolerance. Start by choosing veggies you like to eat, then look into their sizes and care needs.

- **Productivity**

  Think about how much you and your family will eat and how likely you are to freeze, can, or give away excess produce. Then be realistic about how many seeds or plants you need to put into the ground. (Many beginners make the mistake of planting too much.) Vegetables like tomatoes, peppers, and squash keep providing throughout the season, so you may not need many plants to serve your needs. Other vegetables, such as carrots, radishes, and corn, can be harvested only once and then would need to be replanted.

3. Choose the Spot for Your Garden

No matter where you put your garden or what you decide to plant, there are two basic requirements that your location needs to meet for the best success: water and light.

- **Lots of Sunlight Is a Must**

  Like all plants, vegetables need the sun to kick-start photosynthesis. The fastest-growing vegetables need full sun (at least 6 to 8 hours of direct sunlight a day) without blockage from trees, shrubs, or fences. That's why you won't have much success if you plant sun-loving vegetables in shady spaces. If your yard provides partial shade, plant vegetables and herbs that tolerate those conditions, such as lettuce, kale, chard, spinach, chives, cilantro, parsley, and thyme. Root vegetables like carrots, radishes, and beets might also work if your site gets at least 4 hours of direct sunlight a day. Or, if you have a sunny patio, switch to container gardening. That way, you can place sun-loving vegetables and herbs such as tomatoes, cucumbers, beans, basil, dill, and rosemary, where they'll do well.

- ### Think about Convenient Water Access

The closer you can site your plot to a water source, the better. You'll need to be able to water frequently during the first few weeks after seeds germinate or seedlings are transplanted to help these fragile plants produce strong roots and stems. Once your plants are established, it's better to give your garden a long drink every few days rather than a little sprinkle every day. Then the water will move deeper into the soil, which encourages roots to grow deeper, where they're better able to access nutrients they need to stay healthy. Consider installing soaker hoses or drip irrigation on a timer to help minimize water waste and the time you need to spend watering.

4. Plan Your Vegetable Garden Layout

Choose either row cropping or intensive cropping (there are benefits to each!) when you plan your vegetable garden's layout.

- ### Row Cropping

Place plants single file in rows at least 18 inches apart so you can walk easily between them. This approach makes the most sense for large vegetable gardens because rows make it easier to use mechanical equipment, such as tillers, to battle weeds. The downside is that space set aside for footpaths cuts down on the number of vegetables you can plant.

Intensive Cropping

Boost your garden's productivity with intensive cropping, which means that you space two or three plants close together in a bed about 4 feet wide (aka a wide row). Seeds are sown, or transplants are placed so that their leaves will barely touch at maturity. This approach, which uses almost every square inch of the prepared soil, works well for most types of vegetables, excluding the ones that vine (such as cucumbers). The downside of this method is that you have to weed by hand because the plants grow so close together.

5. Start Plants in Rich Soil

For the best harvest, your vegetable garden needs the best soil you can give it. When you feel it, rich, healthy soil is something you know: It's easy to dig and drains well. Pick up a trowel's worth and put it in your hands. Does it feel gritty? Too much sand. Is it powdery? Too much silt. Is it sticky when wet? Too much clay. The combination of these three types, and in which specific proportions, determines the texture of your garden soil. That texture affects drainage and the availability of nutrients.

You want soil that is dark, crumbly, and literally full of life. Fortunately, no matter what the texture may be, all soil can be improved over time by incorporating organic matter into it. Take sandy soils, for instance. They're made up of large soil particles, so water and nutrients run through gaps relatively quickly.

To prepare your soil for planting, spread any needed amendments like compost and work them into the soil with a tiller or spade. Avoid stepping on freshly tilled soil, or you'll compact it and undo all your hard work. Then rake the surface smooth and water thoroughly. Allow the bed to rest several days before you plant so the soil amendments can do their work.

6. Be Ready for Pests and Diseases

Some problems require special solutions, but generally, follow these guidelines to keep pests away from your veggies.

- ### Stop Weeds in Their Tracks

  Weeds compete with your vegetables for light, water, and nutrients, so it's important to keep them to a minimum. A mulch of clean straw, compost, or plastic can keep weeds at bay around larger plants like tomatoes. Use a hoe to discourage any weed seedlings that do pop up.

- ### Keep Animals Out

  Big pests, such as deer and rabbits, can wreak havoc in an edible garden. It takes an 8-foot-tall fence to keep deer from jumping into the garden. A fence needs to extend 6 inches beneath the soil to stop rabbits and other burrowing critters from digging their way in.

- ### Deter Destructive Insects

  Picking off large insects and caterpillars by hand (and dropping them into a bucket of sudsy water) is a safe, effective way to deal with limited infestations. For larger quantities of insects, try insecticidal soap sprays that you can find at most garden centers. Whichever pest-control chemicals you use, carefully follow the manufacturers' directions.

- **Fight Fungal Diseases**

Reduce the likelihood of fungal diseases by watering the soil, not the leaves of the plants. If you use a sprinkler, do it early in the day so the leaves will dry by nightfall. If a plant falls prey to disease, promptly remove it and throw it in the trash; don't add sick plants to your compost pile.

CHAPTER 4

DAY 1

Discover Monday

Monday offers an opportunity to "reset" and get back on track after any lapses over the weekend, and studies show people who get back on track at the beginning of the week are better able to maintain progress over time. Meatless Monday can make a big difference for your health and the health of our planet. Replacing meat with plant-based choices each Monday can offer numerous health benefits and help you take action against climate change by reducing your carbon footprint and helping you conserve precious environmental resources.

Seeds and Nuts Breakfast Bars

High in protein and fiber, these energy bars make for a simple breakfast on the go or an energy-boosting midday snack! Because they are full of little scrubbing seeds, they do a great job of keeping one regular.

Prep time: 5 minutes Servings: 8 bars

Ingredients:

- ▶ ½ cup whole almonds
- ▶ 1 cup almonds sliced
- ▶ ½ cup pecans coarsely chopped
- ▶ 1 cup walnuts coarsely chopped
- ▶ ½ cup sunflower seeds
- ▶ ½ cup sesame seeds
- ▶ ¼ cup flax seed ground
- ▶ 2 tablespoons chia seeds

- 3 tablespoons coconut oil
- 4 tablespoons maple syrup
- 1 cup dried cherries
- 2 tablespoons maple
- ½ teaspoon salt
- 1 teaspoon vanilla

Directions:

- Preheat oven to 120°C/ 250°F.
- Grease an 8-inch square baking pan; line the pan with parchment paper extending over 2 edges of the pan. Set aside.
- Add the cherries, maple, 2 tablespoons coconut oil, salt, and vanilla to the food processor.
- Run the processor until the mixture is fairly smooth.
- In a kadhai/wok, put the nuts roast till crunchy.
- Add the 3 tablespoons of coconut oil and maple syrup. Mix well.
- In a big bowl, combine toasted nut mixture and cherry mixture.
- Work in the cherry mixture in the nuts till well mixed and there are no large chunks left. (Since this is easy if the nuts don't cool).
- Transfer mixture to prepared pan and, using a lightly oiled flat bowl or oiled fingers, pat mixture firmly to an even layer.
- Place pan in the oven.
- Bake for 50-60 minutes or until the bars are no longer sticky.
- Cool in pan, then remove (with parchment paper "handles") to a cutting board and cut into the desired size.
- Store in an airtight container.

Nutrition Facts:

- *Calories: 486kcal*
- *Carbohydrates: 26g*
- *Protein: 11g*

- *Fat: 41g*
- *Saturated Fat: 8g*
- *Sodium: 162mg*
- *Potassium: 414mg*
- *Fiber: 7.6g*
- *Sugar: 16g*
- *Vitamin C: 1mg*
- *Calcium: 110mg*
- *Iron: 3mg*

Avocado, Kale, and Tempeh Salad

Whether you're at the office or exploring the great outdoors, summer and salads are a delightful and logical match. They're light, refreshing, and won't weigh you down. A well-crafted salad will also keep you satiated and give you a good amount of energy. This Kale Avocado Salad with Seasoned Tempeh accomplishes just that!

This time of year is abundant with fresh, flavorful, in-season produce, which makes a salad the perfect summer dish.

Prep time: 10 minutes Servings: 3 servings

Step 1: Preparing Your Mise en Place

- ▶ 1 cup Creamy Lemon Garlic Dressing
- ▶ For this lemon dressing ~ 1 cup
- ▶ ½ cup canned cashews, drained and rinsed
- ▶ ¼ cup lemon juice
- ▶ ¼ cup water
- ▶ 1 clove garlic minced
- ▶ 1 teaspoon apple cider vinegar
- ▶ 1 teaspoon Dijon mustard
- ▶ ½ teaspoon onion powder
- ▶ ½ teaspoon sea salt
- ▶ ¼ cup loosely packed fresh parsley
- ▶ 1 tablespoon fresh thyme
- ▶ Blend all in a food processor. Serving size is about 2 tablespoons2 cups baby kale (or regular kale torn into bite-sized pieces)
- ▶ 2 cups baby spinach
- ▶ 1 cup butter lettuce, torn into bite-sized pieces
- ▶ 1 cup cooked chickpeas
- ▶ 5 to 8 radishes, thinly sliced
- ▶ 2 avocado, thinly sliced

First, prepare the creamy lemon garlic dressing if you don't already have some in your refrigerator. Also, note that other dressings can be used for this salad; for example, this Casper Lemon Dressing would go well with this salad, as would this No-Oil Ranch Dressing; however, this creamy lemon garlic dressing goes particularly well with this salad.

Note: The amount of each ingredient needed depends on how many people you are serving and whether or not you are serving this salad as a main or as an appetizer. Also, feel free to play around with different lettuces — although this combination does work well together. The butter lettuce is used for added color, but it can be omitted if desired.

Step 2: Braising & Frying the Tempeh

- ▶ 1 - 200 gr pkg tempeh
- ▶ 3 to 4 tbsp barbecue sauce
- ▶ 1 tsp oil

Note: Braising the Tempeh is optional. If you do not want to braise the Tempeh, simply dice it up and toss it with the barbecue sauce and then proceed with frying it.

To braise the Tempeh, place the block of Tempeh into a pot just big enough to fit the Tempeh and then add a flavorful stock or liquid, such as soy sauce mixed with water and spices. The liquid should just cover the Tempeh.

Next, bring the mixture to a gentle boil and then reduce the heat and let gently simmer for approximately 15 minutes.

Once done, turn off the heat and let cool slightly. Once the Tempeh is cool enough to handle, cut into approximately 1"-inch pieces and then toss it with the barbecue sauce.

To fry the Tempeh, either dry-sauté or add a touch of oil to a non-stick frypan and sauté until golden brown on most sides. Be careful as the sugar from the barbecue sauce can easily burn Tempeh.

Once done, set aside while you assemble the salad.

Step 3: Assembling the Salad

- ▶ sea salt, to taste
- ▶ freshly ground black pepper, to taste

To assemble the salad, first, toss the lettuces with approximately half of the dressing. Again, the amount will depend on how much lettuce you have, etc. The lettuces should be thoroughly coated in the end. Season lightly with salt and pepper.

Place a good handful of the salad onto a dinner plate and then garnish the plate with the remaining ingredients. Lastly, slice the avocado and then scoop out a few pieces and place them onto each plate.

Nutritions:

- ► *Calories: 506*
- ► *Fat: 30g*
- ► *Saturated Fat: 5g*
- ► *Sodium: 232mg*
- ► *Potassium: 1522mg*
- ► *Carbohydrates: 45g*
- ► *Fiber: 16g*
- ► *Sugar: 11g*
- ► *Protein: 23g*
- ► *Vitamin C: 76mg*
- ► *Calcium: 218mg*
- ► *Iron: 6mg Nutrition info per 1 cup of Lemon dressing or 5 servings Calories: 163*
- ► *Fat: 14g*
- ► *Saturated Fat: 3g*
- ► *Sodium: 322mg*
- ► *Potassium: 154mg*
- ► *Carbohydrates: 9g*
- ► *Fiber: 1g*
- ► *Sugar: 3g*
- ► *Protein: 3g*
- ► *Vitamin C: 10mg*
- ► *Calcium: 26mg*
- ► *Iron: 1.6mg*

Korean BBQ Tacos

This recipe for Korean BBQ Tacos is marinated and impossible meat layered with cabbage slaw and marinated cucumbers, all tucked into warm flour tortillas. A unique take on taco night that's a real crowd pleaser!

This Korean BBQ taco recipe is unexpected but easy to make.

Prep time: 25 minutes Servings: 12 servings

Ingredients:

Beef:

- ▶ 300 g impossible meat
- ▶ 60 ml soy sauce
- ▶ 2 tbsp caster sugar
- ▶ 2 tbsp rice wine vinegar
- ▶ 1 tbsp sesame oil
- ▶ 1 tsp dried chili flakes
- ▶ 2 cloves of garlic

Radish Salad:

- ▶ 60 g radishes (about 7 large (1" to 1-1/4" dia)
- ▶ 1 carrot
- ▶ 1 pear
- ▶ 1 tbsp rice wine vinegar
- ▶ 1/2 clove of garlic, crushed
- ▶ 1 tbsp toasted sesame seeds
- ▶ 1 tbsp caster sugar

Spinach Salad:

- ▶ 100 g fresh spinach (about 3.5 cups)
- ▶ 2 spring onions
- ▶ 1 tbsp toasted sesame seeds
- ▶ 1 tsp sesame oil

To Serve:

- ▶ 6 flour tortillas
- ▶ 4 tbsp Vegan mayonnaise
- ▶ 1 tbsp sriracha sauce

Directions:

Step 1: Marinate the Impossible vegan steak

▶ Slice the Impossible vegan steak into thin slices. Crush the garlic cloves and add to a bowl. Chuck in all the other marinade ingredients, then add the sliced Impossible vegan steak. Marinate for at least 2 hours in the fridge, if not overnight.

Step 2: Radish Salad

▶ Peel and slice the radish, carrot, and pear into very thin strips. Add in the vinegar, sugar, chili flakes, garlic, and sesame seeds, and mix well until there is an even color throughout the salad.

Step 3: Spinach Salad

▶ Wash and finely slice the spring onions. Blanch the spinach in boiling water for 5 seconds, then cool and squeeze dry before tossing with the other ingredients.

Step 4: Sear the Impossible vegan strips

▶ Get two frying pans very hot. Add the strips to one, without too much of marinating liquid, and sear quickly for a minute on each side. In the other frying pan, place the tortillas down one at a time and warm in the dry pan to heat, and start to blacken.

Step 5: Assemble

▶ Mix the mayo and Sriracha, then spread it over the tortillas. Fill the tortillas with spinach, Impossible vegan and top with radish salad to serve. Each tortilla present 2 servings

Nutritions:

- ► *169kcal*
- ► *Carbohydrates: 20g*
- ► *Protein: 8g*
- ► *Fat: 6g*
- ► *Saturated Fat: 1g*
- ► *Cholesterol: 0mg*
- ► *Sodium: 805mg*
- ► *Fiber: 2g*
- ► *Sugar: 5g*

Pan Seared Tempeh Steak with Roasted Broccoli

Broccoli steaks roasted with Pan Seared Tempeh sauce are going to be your new favorite side dish. Crunchy charred broccoli with nutty pistachios and a creamy sauce.

Roasted broccoli is the cat's pajamas – hands down, the best way to make a veggie ever. The stalks get crunchy while the tips are nicely charred and browned with the best smoky taste ever. Roasted broccoli steaks are the way to go.

Prep Time: 5 minutes Servings: 3 servings

Ingredients:

- ▶ ½ cup (120 ml) cold vegetable broth
- ▶ 2 teaspoons cornstarch
- ▶ ¼ cup (60 ml) tamari

- ▶ 3 tablespoons hoisin sauce
- ▶ 2 tablespoons rice wine vinegar
- ▶ 1 tablespoon Sriracha sauce
- ▶ 1 pound (455 g) tempeh, sliced on a diagonal
- ▶ 3 tablespoons toasted sesame oil
- ▶ 1 cup (115 g) thinly sliced shallots
- ▶ 6 cups (540 g) broccoli florets
- ▶ 2 tablespoons minced fresh ginger
- ▶ 2 cloves garlic, minced

Directions:

- ▶ In a mug using a fork, mix the broth and cornstarch until well dissolved. Add the tamari, hoisin, rice wine vinegar, and Sriracha. Set the sauce aside.
- ▶ Preheat a large skillet over medium-high heat. Cook the Tempeh in 1 tablespoon of the sesame oil until seared on both sides, 7 to 10 minutes. Transfer the Tempeh to a plate and set it aside.
- ▶ Add 1 tablespoon of the sesame oil to the skillet and cook the broccoli, often stirring, until softened, about 5 minutes.
- ▶ Push the broccoli to the side and add the ginger and garlic to a clear spot. Drizzle the remaining tablespoon of sesame oil on the ginger and garlic and toss for about 30 seconds, just until fragrant, and then toss the aromatics together with the broccoli.
- ▶ Return the Tempeh to the pan. Pour in the reserved sauce, mix everything together, and increase the heat to bring it to a boil. Let the sauce thicken and reduce for about 3 minutes, then lower the heat and cook for another 2 minutes. Serve over rice, garnished with sesame seeds, scallions, and sliced dried pepper, if desired.

Nutritions:

- ▶ *Calories: 394*

- ▶ *Fat: 18g*
- ▶ *Saturated Fat: 4g*
- ▶ *Protein: 35g*
- ▶ *Carbohydrates: 29g*
- ▶ *Fiber: 4g*
- ▶ *Iron: 7mg*
- ▶ *Sodium: 1578mg*
- ▶ *Calcium: 279mg*

Motivational Tips On Preserving the Food and Reusing the Food:

The best time-saving device is giving it time to read recipes before anything else. It provides more accurate measurement and comprehension of methods from the start. Especially when you are not familiar with the recipe. When you don't know a procedure, you can still search and ask around how to do it instead of dealing with it when it's already in front of you.

CHAPTER 5:

DAY 2

TuesdayForEmpoweredGreens

The Vegan Diet outlines a weight-loss plan with "no animal products, no fast food, no processed food, plenty of high-fiber natural foods, fruits and vegetables, and soy products. The Vegan Diet is an elimination diet. Its creators encourage people to remove all animal products from their diets to achieve weight loss and to be healthier.

Zucchini and Cauliflower Fritters

These zucchini and cauliflower fritters are the perfect lunchbox or after-school treat, and they're great for toddlers too. With a crunchy outside and a delicious center, the kids won't be able to get enough of these!

Prep time: 20 minutes Servings: 24 pcs.

Ingredients:

► 600 g cauliflower (leaves removed, cut into florets)
► 1 clove garlic (slightly crushed)
► 1 tsp onion flakes
► 1 medium zucchini (grated)
► 1 cup Vegan parmesan cheese (finely grated)
► 1/4 cup tasty Vegan cheese (grated)
► 2 cups self-raising flour
► 1 pinch salt and pepper
► 2 Tbsp of egg raplacment
► 3/4 cup water
► 1 splash olive oil

Direction:

► Place the cauliflower florets into a food processor and blitz until they turn into small pieces. Transfer to a large bowl.
► Add the crushed garlic, onion flakes, grated zucchini,Vegan parmesan cheese, and tasty cheese to the bowl with the cauliflower, sift over the self-raising flour and stir to combine.
► Add the salt and pepper, then the egg powder replacer along with 1/4 cup of water to the bowl with the cauliflower mixture, and stir to combine. Gradually add the extra water and stir until you have a thick batter.
► Place a tablespoon of olive oil into a large frying pan and heat over medium/high heat. Use a 1/4 measuring cup to scoop up the batter

and place approximately six fritters (you may fit more in depending on the size of your pan) into your frying pan. Gently spread/flatten the fritters with a spoon until they are between 1/2cm-1cm thick.

▶ Cook the fritters for 5 minutes on each side until they are crisp and golden brown before transferring to a plate and covering them with foil while you cook the next batch. Repeat the above step until all the fritters have been cooked, and then serve the fritters warm with a dollop of Vegan sour cream or tomato relish.

Nutrition per piece:

▶ *Calories: 92kcal*
▶ *Carbohydrates: 18g*
▶ *Protein: 5g*
▶ *Fat: 1g*
▶ *Saturated Fat: 0g*
▶ *Sodium: 15mg*
▶ *Potassium: 267mg*
▶ *Fiber: 0g*
▶ *Sugar: 0g*
▶ *Calcium: 25mg*
▶ *Iron: 1.5mg*

Ginger Avocado Kale Salad

This happy, feel-good kale salad recipe is packed with colorful vegetables. Great for lunch! The most delicious kale salad ever! This is an easy, massaged kale avocado salad with a simple soy, ginger, and sesame dressing.

Prep time: 15 minutes Servings: 4 servings

Ingredients:

Salad:

- ► 1 small bunch kale, chopped ~ 1 lbs.
- ► 1 tbsp lime juice
- ► 1/4 tsp salt
- ► 2 avocados, diced
- ► 1 large carrot, peeled and grated

Ginger Soy Dressing:

- ▶ 2 tbsp sesame oil
- ▶ 1 tbsp lime juice
- ▶ 1 tbsp soy sauce
- ▶ 1 tsp grated ginger
- ▶ 1 small clove garlic, grated

Directions:

- ▶ In a large bowl, toss kale with 1 tbsp of lime juice and 1/4 tsp of salt. Massage kale with your hands, crunching between your fingers until kale becomes darker green and tender, about 1-2 minutes. Stir in avocado and grated carrot.
- ▶ For the dressing, whisk sesame oil with lime juice, soy sauce, ginger, and garlic in a small bowl. Add dressing to salad and toss to serve.

Nutrition

- ▶ *Calories: 294kcal*
- ▶ *Carbohydrates: 23g*
- ▶ *Protein: 8g*
- ▶ *Fat: 23g*
- ▶ *Saturated Fat: 3g*
- ▶ *Sodium: 460mg*
- ▶ *Potassium: 1142mg*
- ▶ *Fiber: 11.5g*
- ▶ *Sugar: 4g*
- ▶ *Calcium: 194mg*
- ▶ *Iron: 2.4mg*

Guacamole

Guacamole has a role in the kitchen beyond a party dip. It's great scooped on top of nachos and also makes an excellent topping or side for enchiladas, tacos, grilled salmon, or oven-baked chicken. Guacamole is great in foods, as well.

The trick to making perfect guacamole is using avocados that are just the right amount of ripeness. Not ripe enough, and the avocado will be hard and flavorless. Too ripe, and the taste will be off.

Prep time: 10 minutes Servings: 4 servings

Ingredients:

- ► 2 ripe avocados
- ► 1/4 teaspoon salt, plus more to taste
- ► 1 tablespoon fresh lime or lemon juice
- ► 3 tablespoons minced red onion or thinly sliced green onion

- ▶ 1-2 serrano (or jalapeño) chilis, stems and seeds removed, minced
- ▶ 2 tablespoons cilantro (leaves and tender stems), finely chopped
- ▶ Pinch freshly ground black pepper
- ▶ 1/2 ripe tomato, chopped (optional)
- ▶ Red radish or jicama slices for garnish (optional)
- ▶ Tortilla chips to serve (10 pcs.per serving)

Directions:

- ▶ Cut the avocados in half. Remove the pit. Score the inside of the avocado with a blunt knife and scoop out the flesh with a spoon.
- ▶ Using a fork, roughly mash the avocado. (Don't overdo it! The guacamole should be a little chunky.)
- ▶ Sprinkle with salt and lime (or lemon) juice. The acid in the lime juice will provide some balance to the richness of the avocado and will help delay the avocados from turning brown.
- ▶ Add the chopped onion, cilantro, black pepper, and chilis. Chili peppers vary individually in their spiciness. So, start with a half of one chili pepper and add more to the guacamole to your desired degree of heat.
- ▶ Remember that much of this is done to taste because of the variability in the fresh ingredients. Start with this recipe and adjust to your taste.
- ▶ If making a few hours ahead, place plastic wrap on the surface of the guacamole and press down to cover it to prevent air from reaching it. (The oxygen in the air causes oxidation which will turn the guacamole brown.)
- ▶ Garnish with slices of red radish or jigama strips. Serve with your choice of store-bought tortilla chips or make your own homemade tortilla chips.
- ▶ Refrigerate leftover guacamole for up to 3 days.

Nutritions:

- ► *Calories: 290kcal*
- ► *Carbohydrates: 26g*
- ► *Protein: 4g*
- ► *Fat: 20g*
- ► *Saturated Fat: 3g*
- ► *Sodium: 232mg*
- ► *Potassium: 596mg*
- ► *Fiber: 8g*
- ► *Sugar: 2g*
- ► *Calcium: 43mg*
- ► *Iron: 1mg*

Smashed Bean Sandwiches

This vegetarian play on tuna salad relies on white beans as the base. The beans become so creamy when smashed that only a touch of mayonnaise is needed to bring it together, and celery seed and tangy lemon juice intensify the flavor. It's ultra-versatile: slather it on thick bread slices as a sandwich, mound it on top of salad greens, or spread it on a croissant for an impressive brunch.

Prep time: 20 minutes Servings: 4 servings

Ingredients:

- ▶ 1 stalk celery
- ▶ 3 small green onions
- ▶ 1 15-ounce of can navy or cannellini beans
- ▶ 1 tablespoon vegan mayonnaise
- ▶ 2 tablespoons lemon juice (1/2 lemon)
- ▶ 3/4 teaspoon celery seed
- ▶ 1/8 teaspoon garlic powder

- 1/4 – 1/2 teaspoon kosher salt
- Freshly ground black pepper
- 4 slices bread or 2 croissants
- 2 radishes
- 2 leaves lettuce

Directions:

- Thinly slice the celery and green onions. Drain and lightly rinse the navy beans.
- In a medium bowl, roughly smash the beans with a fork, leaving about a third of their whole. Stir in the celery, green onions, vegan mayonnaise, lemon juice, celery seed, garlic powder, kosher salt, and several grinds of black pepper. Taste and continue adding kosher salt a few pinches at a time until the flavor pops but is not too salty; the exact amount of salt will vary based on the brand of beans.
- Toast the bread. Thinly slice the radishes. Place lettuce on one slice of bread then spread the bean salad. Top with sliced radishes and the remaining slice of bread.

Nutritions:

- *Calories: 214kcal*
- *Carbohydrates: 39g*
- *Protein: 11g*
- *Fat: 2g*
- *Saturated Fat: 0g*
- *Sodium: 794mg*
- *Potassium: 439mg*
- *Fiber: 7g*
- *Sugar: 3g*
- *Calcium: 115mg*
- *Iron: 3.5mg*

Motivational Tips on Preserving the Food and Reusing the Food

Pantry staples that are most essential are sugar, salt, and acid. Salt may include sea salt, rock salt, Himalayan salt, tamari, low-sodium soy sauce, or miso. For sugar, the most advisable ones are brown sugar, coconut sugar, dates, maple syrup, or even applesauce. For acids, fermented veggies are healthful, vinegar, and other citrus juice like lime, lemons, or grapefruit.

CHAPTER 6

DAY 3

Loaded With Fiber Wednesday

E at more fiber. We've all heard this advice, so we assume it must be good for us. The problem is that fiber and flavor might seem like opposites — and for many of us, the flavor is the typical driver of food choice. But the reality is that fiber can have flavor, along with medicinal effects, to help reduce and prevent common diseases potentially.

Bagels with Tahini

bagel tahini sauce has all the punchy garlic and onion flavors in a creamy sesame base with a sprinkle of poppy seeds.

Prep time: 10 minutes Servings: 4 servings

Ingredients:

- ¼ cup tahini, well-stirred & runny
- 1 tablespoon white wine vinegar
- 1 teaspoon maple syrup or agave nectar
- 1½ teaspoons onion powder
- ¾ teaspoon garlic powder
- ¼ cup ice water, plus extra
- sea salt & ground black pepper, to taste
- 1 teaspoon poppy seeds

Directions:

- In a medium bowl, combine the tahini, white wine vinegar, maple syrup, onion powder, and garlic powder. Whisk this mixture until you have a thick paste. Then, slowly add the ice water in 1 tablespoon increments, whisking the sauce after each addition. Once you have a fluid, pale, and creamy consistency, you're good! Add more cold water if necessary. Then, season the sauce with salt and pepper and stir in the poppy seeds.
- This sauce is best after storing in the fridge for a few hours. It keeps in a sealed container in the fridge for about a week!

Nutritions:

- *Calories: 102*
- *Fat: 8g*
- *Saturated Fat: 1g*

- ► *Sodium: 45mg*
- ► *Carbohydrates: 6g*
- ► *Fiber: 1g*
- ► *Sugars: 1g*
- ► *Protein: 3g*
- ► *Potassium: 94mg*
- ► *Calcium: 37mg*
- ► *Iron: 1mg*

Buffalo Jackfruit Tacos

Weeknight dinners just don't get easier than these jackfruit tacos! Just cook the jackfruit in a skillet with spicy Buffalo sauce, add your toppings, and go! You can serve the jackfruit in a taco shell or a soft taco, top with whatever veggies you desire. The whole dish has great aesthetic appeal, can be thrown together in minutes with minimal effort, has the classic heat of the Buffalo sauce and the coolness of the vegan blue cheese, and is perfect for entertaining.

Prep time: 15 minutes Servings: 10 servings

Ingredients:

- 6 taco shells
- 1 20-ounce can jackfruit in brine
- 1/2-3/4 cup Buffalo sauce
- 1 cup red cabbage, sliced
- 1 cup white cabbage, sliced
- 2 tablespoons chives, chopped
- Vegan blue cheese, as desired

Directions:

- Drain the jackfruit and add to a saucepan with 3 cups of water, bring to a boil over medium heat and boil for 5 minutes. Drain, shred with a fork, and throw in a pan with Buffalo sauce for 5-7 minutes on medium to high heat.
- The jackfruit should take on a slightly darker color. Remove from heat and dress your tacos in cabbage mix, avocado, and top with blue cheese and chives.

Nutritions:

- *Calories: 123kcal*
- *Carbohydrates: 26g*
- *Fat: 2g*
- *Sodium: 215mg*
- *Potassium: 144mg*
- *Vitamin C: 7mg*
- *Calcium: 45mg*
- *Iron: 0.5mg*

Multi-Seed Crackers

Turn leftover brown rice and quinoa from dinner or meal-prepping into these delicious crispy crackers that are loaded with three good-for-you seeds--and create an everything-bagel flavor without the bagel. The whole grains that make up this copycat cracker recipe add lots of fiber for a healthy snack that pairs perfectly with hummus or cheese.

Prep time: 15 minutes Servings: 20 servings

Ingredients:

- ▶ 1 cup cooked brown rice, at room temperature
- ▶ 1 cup cooked quinoa, at room temperature
- ▶ ¼ cup sesame seeds
- ▶ ¼ cup flaxseeds
- ▶ ¼ cup sunflower seeds
- ▶ 2 tablespoons reduced-sodium tamari

- ► 2 tablespoons water
- ► ¼ teaspoon salt
- ► ¼ teaspoon ground pepper

Directions:

- ► Place oven racks in the upper and lower sections of the oven. Preheat to 350 degrees F. Cut 3 pieces of parchment paper the size of a large baking sheet.
- ► Place rice, quinoa, sesame seeds, flaxseeds, sunflower seeds, tamari, water, salt, and pepper in a food processor. Process until finely chopped and coming together in a ball. The dough will be sticky.
- ► Divide the dough in half. Place 1 piece of dough between 2 sheets of the prepared parchment paper. Roll out as thin as possible. Remove the top sheet of parchment and place the dough with parchment on a baking sheet. Repeat with the remaining dough and prepared parchment.
- ► Bake for 15 minutes. Switch the position of the baking sheets and continue baking until dark around the edges and crisp, 12 to 15 minutes more. Remove from oven and carefully break into roughly shaped crackers. If some crackers aren't fully crisp, return them to the oven and bake for 5 to 10 minutes more.
- ► To make ahead: Store crackers in an airtight container for up to 1 week.

Nutritions:

- ► *Calories: 56kcal*
- ► *Carbohydrates: 5g*
- ► *Protein: 2g*
- ► *Fat: 3g*
- ► *Saturated Fat: 0.3g*
- ► *Sodium: 132mg*

► *Potassium: 60mg*
► *Fiber: 1g*
► *Sugar: 0g*
► *Vitamin C: 0mg*
► *Calcium: 11mg*
► *Iron: 1mg*

Black Bean Burgers

Whether you're vegetarian or not, this black bean burger recipe will hit every spot. Made with black beans, oats, onion, and carrots and spiced up with cumin, coriander, and cayenne, this burger is so good you'll wonder whether you ever want to go back to the carnivore version. Cook the patties on a pan covered in cooking spray, or use a slightly more generous pour of cooking oil for a crispier finish.

Prep time: 15 minutes Servings: 6 servings

Ingredients:

- ▶ 2 cans black beans, rinsed and drained
- ▶ 1 onion, minced
- ▶ 3 cloves garlic, minced
- ▶ 2 carrots, shredded
- ▶ ½ cup quick-cook oats(50g)

- ▶ 1 tablespoon soy sauce
- ▶ 1 tablespoon olive oil
- ▶ 1 teaspoon cumin
- ▶ ½ teaspoon coriander
- ▶ ½ teaspoon chili powder
- ▶ ¼ teaspoon cayenne pepper
- ▶ salt, to taste
- ▶ pepper, to taste
- ▶ 6 buns

Directions:

- ▶ Heat one tablespoon of olive oil in a pan. Combine onions, garlic, salt, and pepper and cook until onions are translucent.
- ▶ Add carrots, cumin, coriander, chili powder, and cayenne pepper until carrots are tender. Remove pan from heat.
- ▶ In a bowl, mash the beans and then add the contents of the pan along with the soy sauce and quick oats.
- ▶ Mix and form four patties. Place in the freezer for 30 minutes to set.
- ▶ Cook patties on a pan coated in cooking spray over medium heat, flipping halfway.
- ▶ Use patties to create your dream veggie burger.

Nutritions:

- ▶ *Calories: 395kcal*
- ▶ *Carbohydrates: 53g*
- ▶ *Protein: 11g*
- ▶ *Fat: 16g*
- ▶ *Saturated Fat: 6g*
- ▶ *Sodium: 354mg*
- ▶ *Potassium: 368mg*
- ▶ *Fiber: 8g*

- *Sugar: 15g*
- *Vitamin C: 4mg*
- *Calcium: 118mg*
- *Iron: 3mg*

Motivational Tips On Preserving the Food and Reusing the Food

Pantry staples that are most essential are sugar, salt, and acid. Salt may include sea salt, rock salt, Himalayan salt, tamari, low-sodium soy sauce, or miso. For sugar, the most advisable ones are brown sugar, coconut sugar, dates, maple syrup, or even applesauce. For acids, fermented veggies are healthful, vinegar, and other citrus juice like lime, lemons, or grapefruit.

CHAPTER 7

DAY 4

Motivated With Tomatoes And Tofu

For women experiencing menopause, tofu may be a great option to include in the diet. Tofu contains a group of phytoestrogen chemicals found in plant foods called isoflavones. These isoflavones have a similar structure to the hormone estrogen, meaning they mimic the action of estrogen produced by the body, naturally binding to receptor sites in human cells.

High-Protein Quinoa Bowl

This delicious dish is a great post-gym meal. Packed with color and texture, it's a bowl full of goodness!

Prep time: 10 minutes Servings: 6 servings

Ingredients:

To make the quinoa:

▶ 1 ½ cups quinoa rinsed well
▶ 3 cups water or vegetable broth
▶ 1 teaspoon salt
▶ 1 tablespoon Peanut butter spread

To make the power bowl:

▶ 3 tablespoons Peanut butter spread divided
▶ 1 package of Gardein Classic Meatless Meatballs ~ 16 oz

- ► 1 cup fresh corn
- ► 12 stalks of asparagus rinsed and cut into small (1 inch pieces)
- ► ¼ teaspoon salt
- ► Pinch of black pepper
- ► 1 cup scallions chopped
- ► 2 tablespoons lemon juice
- ► ½ cup sprouts or salad greens
- ► ½ cup red cabbage chopped
- ► 1 ripe avocado cut into small cubes
- ► 6 baby bell peppers
- ► Drizzle of olive oil optional

Directions:

- ► Put the quinoa and water in a pot and cover with a lid. Bring to the boil, then remove the lid so the steam can escape. Simmer until all the water has been absorbed. Remove the pot from the heat, cover it with the lid again, and set aside for 5 to 10 minutes until the quinoa is fully cooked. Fluff up with a fork.
- ► Meanwhile, put the frozen peas or edamame beans in a heatproof bowl, cover with just-boiled water, and set aside for 10 minutes to thaw.
- ► Put all the dressing ingredients in a cup or jug and whisk together with a fork.
- ► To serve, divide the cooked quinoa between four bowls. Evenly divide the thawed peas or edamame beans, mixed salad leaves, cherry tomatoes, nuts, and fresh herbs between the bowls, then drizzle over the dressing. However, if you're making this ahead of time or eating over the next couple of days, store the bowl ingredients and dress separately, and add the dressing just before serving, as it will keep better this way.

Nutritions:

- ► *Calories: 533kcal*
- ► *Carbohydrates: 67g*
- ► *Protein: 28g*
- ► *Fat: 19g*
- ► *Saturated Fat: 3g*
- ► *Sodium: 1205mg*
- ► *Potassium: 936mg*
- ► *Fiber: 14g*
- ► *Sugar: 7g*
- ► *Vitamin C: 107mg*
- ► *Calcium: 78mg*
- ► *Iron: 6mg*

Roasted Vegetables, Tofu, and Pumpkin Salad

Crispy tofu lends protein to this burrito bowl-inspired veggie-packed grain bowl that's perfect for a quick and easy dinner or packable lunch for work.

Prep time: 20 minutes Servings: 4 servings

Ingredients:

- 8 ounces extra-firm tofu, cut into 1-inch cubes
- 5 tablespoons plus 1 teaspoon extra-virgin olive oil, divided
- 1 tablespoon reduced-sodium tamari or soy sauce (see Tip)
- ½ teaspoon chili powder
- 1 medium red bell pepper, cut into 1/2-inch strips
- ½ medium red onion, cut into 1/2-inch wedges
- ½ avocado

- ⅓ cup water
- ¼ cup packed cilantro leaves, plus more for garnish
- 2 tablespoons lime juice
- ½ teaspoon ground coriander
- ¼ teaspoon salt
- 1 cup cooked brown rice
- ½ cup chopped romaine lettuce
- 6 cherry tomatoes, halved
- 2 tablespoons toasted pumpkin seeds

Directions:

- Preheat oven to 425 degrees F. Line a rimmed baking sheet with parchment paper.
- Toss tofu, 1 tablespoon oil, tamari (or soy sauce), and chili powder in a medium bowl. Place on one side of the prepared baking sheet. Add pepper, onion, and 1 teaspoon oil to the bowl; stir to coat. Place the vegetables on the other side of the baking sheet. Roast until the vegetables are tender and the tofu is sizzling for about 20 minutes.
- Meanwhile, combine the remaining 4 tablespoons of oil, avocado, water, cilantro, lime juice, coriander, and salt in a blender jar or mini food processor. Process until smooth, scraping the sides down as necessary.
- Place 1/2 cup rice in each of 2 shallow serving bowls. Top with tofu, roasted vegetables, lettuce, and tomatoes. Spoon 4 tablespoons dressing over each bowl and sprinkle with pumpkin seeds.

Nutritions:

- *Calories: 340kcal*
- *Carbohydrates: 19g*
- *Protein: 9g*
- *Fat: 27g*

- ► *Saturated Fat: 3g*
- ► *Sodium: 182mg*
- ► *Potassium: 408mg*
- ► *Fiber: 4g*
- ► *Sugar: 3g*
- ► *Vitamin C: 47mg*
- ► *Calcium: 123mg*
- ► *Iron: 2mg*

Tip: People with celiac disease or **gluten** sensitivity should use soy sauces that are labeled «gluten-free,» as soy sauce may contain wheat or other gluten-containing sweeteners and flavors.

Sage Pecan Cauliflower

Cauliflower always seems to have the answers. Need a fruit-free smoothie? Throw frozen cauliflower in it. Need a grain-free pizza crust? Shred some cauliflower. A vegan cheese sauce? Puree that cauliflower with some Nutritions: al yeast, and voila!

While cauliflower does an incomparable job as a stealth-food chameleon, it also deserves to be celebrated exactly as-is—whole, unabashed in its full glory.

Prep time: 25 minutes Servings: 4 servings

Ingredients:

- ▶ 1 head of cauliflower – remove florets from the head and slice into bite-size chunks
- ▶ 1 small onion, diced
- ▶ 1 medium shallot, diced

- ► 1/3 cup pecans, chopped
- ► 3 tablespoons olive oil
- ► 1 tablespoon sherry vinegar
- ► 1 tablespoon fresh lemon juice
- ► a handful of fresh curly parsley, chopped
- ► 10 fresh sage leaves, diced
- ► season liberally with salt and pepper (I also like to use a little Montreal Steak Seasoning and Bologna Herbal Salt Blend)

Directions:

- ► Preheat oven to 450
- ► Whisk together oil, vinegar, parsley, sage, and seasoning in a large bowl. Add cauliflower, shallot, onion, and pecans to the bowl and toss until coated thoroughly.
- ► Spread veggies on a deep dish baking sheet or in a roasting pan. Roast for 25 minutes, stirring to rotate a few times periodically, until fork tender.

Nutritions:

- ► *Calories: 213kcal*
- ► *Carbohydrates: 15g*
- ► *Protein: 5g*
- ► *Fat: 17g*
- ► *Saturated Fat: 2g*
- ► *Sodium: 66mg*
- ► *Potassium: 727mg*
- ► *Fiber: 6g*
- ► *Sugar: 6g*
- ► *Vitamin C: 108mg*
- ► *Calcium: 65mg*
- ► *Iron: 2mg*

Garlic Lemon Mushrooms

Lemon Garlic Mushrooms are a fantastic side dish or appetizer. This mushroom recipe is beyond simple and goes with just about any meal. The bright and tangy lemon flavor shines with the earthy garlic and mushrooms.

Prep time: 10 minutes Servings: 4 servings

Ingredients:

- ▶ 24 ounces Cremini Mushrooms
- ▶ 3 Tablespoons Olive Oil
- ▶ 1 Tablespoon Lemon Juice
- ▶ 4 Garlic Cloves, (grated)
- ▶ Salt/Pepper
- ▶ Parsley
- ▶ Lemon Zest

Directions:

▶ Preheat oven to 400°F

▶ Clean mushrooms with a damp paper towel and trim stems. Toss mushrooms with oil, lemon juice, and garlic cloves. Transfer to a roasting dish or rimmed baking sheet.

▶ Roast for 10 minutes. Toss, then roast for 10-15 minutes more or until desired tenderness.

▶ Remove from oven. Salt and pepper to taste. Sprinkle with fresh parsley and lemon zest to serve.

Nutritions:

▶ *Calories: 133kcal*

▶ *Carbohydrates: 7g*

▶ *Protein: 5g*

▶ *Fat: 11g*

▶ *Saturated Fat: 2g*

▶ *Sodium: 48mg*

▶ *Potassium: 562mg*

▶ *Fiber: 2g*

▶ *Sugar: 3g*

▶ *Vitamin C: 7mg*

▶ *Calcium: 12mg*

▶ Iron: 1mg

Motivational Tips On Preserving the Food and Reusing the Food

Invest in a good chef's knife. A big knife is easier to work with. Longer blades give easier cuts for bigger things like squash. Wider blades can scoop ingredients to make it easier to toss in a dish or pan.

CHAPTER 8

DAY 5

Run With Peanuts And Energize With Eggplants

Almond and Flax Low-Carb Muffins

Flax low-carb muffins are satisfying, filling keto breakfast for any day of the week. Make ahead or freeze and have these low-carb pumpkin pecan flax muffins whenever you're hungry for a snack or meal!

Prep time: 10 minutes Servings: 9 muffins

Ingredients:

- 1 ¼ cup ground golden flaxseed
- 1 tablespoon coconut flour
- ½ teaspoon gluten-free baking soda
- 3 tablespoons stevia sweetener
- ¾ teaspoon ground cinnamon
- ¼ teaspoon ground cloves
- ¼ teaspoon ground mace and/or ground nutmeg
- ¼ teaspoon pink Himalayan salt
- 1 cup of applesauce⅓ cup olive oil
- ½ cup fresh or canned pumpkin puree
- ¼ cup fullfat coconut cream
- 1 teaspoon vanilla
- 1 teaspoon lemon juice
- ¼ cup chopped pecans, plus more for topping (optional)

Directions:

- Preheat oven to 325°F.
- Stir all dry ingredients together in a large mixing bowl.
- Add the remaining ingredients and stir until completely incorporated.
- Using a silicone muffin pan or a metal muffin pan filled with cupcake liners, fill ¾ full.
- For mini muffins, bake at 325°F for 15-18 minutes. For regular-sized muffins, bake at

- ▶ 325°F for 18-22 minutes.
- ▶ Allow resting for 15 minutes before serving. Serve alone or topped with vegan butter or vegan cream cheese. Makes about 12 regular-sized muffins or 24 mini muffins.

Nutritions:

- ▶ *Calories: 262kcal*
- ▶ *Carbohydrates: 16g*
- ▶ *Protein: 5g*
- ▶ *Fat: 21g*
- ▶ *Saturated Fat: 3g*
- ▶ *Sodium: 147mg*
- ▶ *Potassium: 265mg*
- ▶ *Fiber: 7g*
- ▶ *Sugar: 8g*
- ▶ *Vitamin C: 1mg*
- ▶ *Calcium: 68mg*
- ▶ Iron: 1.6mg

Cabbage Steaks

Cabbage Steaks may sound like an oxymoron, but I guarantee that once you try them, you'll be hooked. Roasted cabbage steaks are a hearty addition to any meal. Try it tonight with some dinner rolls, or with some hot tomato soup this weekend

Prep time: 15 minutes Servings: 5 servings

Ingredients:

- ▶ 1 large head of cabbage
- ▶ 2 tablespoons light olive oil
- ▶ 2 tablespoons minced garlic
- ▶ ½ teaspoon salt, or to taste
- ▶ ½ teaspoon ground black pepper, or to taste

Directions:

▶ Preheat oven to 350 degrees F (175 degrees C).

▶ Cut the bottom off of the cabbage and set it so that the flat end is on the cutting board; cut into 1-inch thick slices. Arrange slices in a single layer in a large casserole dish.

▶ Drizzle olive oil over the cabbage slices and top with garlic. Season cabbage with salt and pepper. Cover the dish with aluminum foil.

▶ Bake in preheated oven until the cabbage core is easily pierced with a fork, about 45 minutes.

Nutritions:

▶ *Calories: 120kcal*

▶ *Carbohydrates: 17g*

▶ *Protein: 3g*

▶ *Fat: 6g*

▶ *Saturated Fat: 1g*

▶ *Sodium: 294mg*

▶ *Potassium: 560mg*

▶ *Fiber: 5g*

▶ *Sugar: 9g*

▶ *Vitamin C: 130mg*

▶ *Calcium: 106mg*

▶ Iron: 2mg

Snickerdoodles

A snickerdoodle cookie has to be soft and chewy. No hard hockey puck cookies here! It has to be rolled twice in cinnamon sugar to ensure that it is completely coated. It also has to have the signature tang from the cream of tartar.

Prep time: 20 minutes Servings: 48 servings

Ingredients:

- ► 1 cup vegan Unsalted Butter (softened)
- ► 1 1/2 cups Sugar
- ► ½ a cup of applesauce2 teaspoons Vanilla
- ► 2 3/4 cup Flour
- ► 1 1/2 teaspoon Cream of Tartar
- ► 1/2 teaspoon Baking Soda
- ► 1 teaspoon Salt

Cinnamon-Sugar Mixture:

- ▶ 1/4 cup Sugar
- ▶ 1 1/2 Tablespoons Cinnamon

Directions:

- ▶ Preheat oven to 350 degrees
- ▶ In a large mixing bowl, cream butter and sugar for 4-5 minutes until light and fluffy.
- ▶ Scrape the sides of the bowl and add the applesauce and vanilla. Cream for 1-2 minutes longer.
- ▶ Stir in flour, cream of tartar, baking soda, and salt, just until combined.
- ▶ In a small bowl, stir together sugar and cinnamon.
- ▶ If time allows, wrap the dough and let refrigerate for 20-30 minutes. Roll into small balls until round and smooth. Drop into the cinnamon-sugar mixture and coat well. Using a spoon, a coat for a second time, ensuring the cookie balls are completely covered. To make flatter snickerdoodles, press down in the center of the ball before placing it in the oven. This helps to keep them from puffing up in the middle.
- ▶ Place on a parchment paper-lined baking sheet. Bake for 9-11 minutes. Let cool for several minutes on the baking sheet before removing it from the pan.

Nutritions:

- ▶ *Calories: 88kcal*
- ▶ *Carbohydrates: 15g*
- ▶ *Protein: 2g*
- ▶ *Fat: 2g*
- ▶ *Saturated Fat: 0g*

► *Sodium: 94mg*

► *Potassium: 67mg*

► *Fiber: 1g*

► *Sugar: 8g*

► *Vitamin C: 0mg*

► *Calcium: 6mg*

► *Iron: 0.5mg*

Vermicelli Stir-Fry with Tofu and Vegetables

Toss up a storm tonight with a wok full of sweet and tasty Thai-style noodles. Coriander and tender-crisp veggies make this speedy stir-fry taste super fresh.

Prep time: 15 minutes Servings: 4 servings

Ingredients:

- ► 1 8-ounce package rice noodles or 12 ounces linguine
- ► ¼ cup brown sugar
- ► ¼ cup low-sodium soy sauce
- ► 2 tablespoons fresh lime juice
- ► 1 14-ounce package firm tofu, cut into 1/2-inch-thick slices
- ► 1 tablespoon canola oil
- ► 2 carrots, cut into thin strips

- 1 red bell pepper, thinly sliced
- 1 tablespoon grated fresh ginger
- 2 cups bean sprouts
- 4 scallions, thinly sliced
- ¼ cup roasted peanuts, roughly chopped
- ½ cup fresh cilantro (optional)

Directions:

- Boil the noodles according to the package directions. Drain and return them to the pot.
- Meanwhile, whisk together the sugar, soy sauce, and lime juice in a small bowl.
- Gently press the tofu slices between layers of paper towels to remove excess liquid, then cut into ½-inch pieces.
- Heat the oil in a large skillet over medium-high heat. Add the carrots, bell pepper, and ginger and cook, stirring, for 2 minutes. Add the tofu and bean sprouts. Cook, stirring, until the vegetables are slightly tender, 3 to 4 minutes.
- Toss the noodles with half the soy sauce mixture and cook over medium-high heat until heated through 1 to 2 minutes. Transfer to a platter and top with the vegetables and the remaining soy sauce mixture.
- Sprinkle with the scallions, peanuts, and cilantro, if desired.

Nutritions:

- *Calories: 397kcal*
- *Carbohydrates: 66g*
- *Protein: 11g*
- *Fat: 10g*
- *Saturated Fat: 2g*
- *Sodium: 712mg*

- *Potassium: 548mg*
- *Fiber: 5g*
- *Sugar: 12g*
- *Vitamin C: 81mg*
- *Calcium: 101mg*
- Iron: 2mg

Motivational Tips On Preserving the Food and Reusing the Food

Vegan cooking is easier than most other cooking. There's no fear of poisoning yourself; in fact, you can eat raw vegetables. Vegetables are easier to cook so that lunch can be made in as fast as 15 minutes.

CHAPTER 9

DAY 6

Tasty Leafs And Beans

Enjoy your day with the nature of tasty Leafs and Beans.

Chia Pudding

Cooking with chia seeds might sound intimidating, but in reality, they couldn't be easier to whip up! Simply add liquid (we like almond milk, but any milk works) and let time do the rest. In a couple of hours, your seeds will be transformed into a creamy, smooth pudding. We like ours topped with fresh fruit and granola, but feel free to go crazy with your favorite toppings! Yogurt, nut butter, and jams are all great mix-ins.

Prep time: 15 minutes Servings: 4 servings

Ingredients:

- 1/4 c. chia seeds
- 1 c. almond milk (or milk of your choice)
- 2 tsp. maple syrup, or agave nectar
- 1 tsp. pure vanilla extract (optional)
- Pinch kosher salt
- Sliced fruit, granola, jam, or nuts for serving (not included in nutrition info)

Directions:

- In a medium bowl, whisk to combine chia seeds, milk, sweetener of your choice, vanilla if using, and salt.
- Cover and refrigerate until thick, 2 hours up to overnight.
- Serve with mix-ins and toppings of your choice.

Nutritions:

- *Calories: 83kcal*
- *Carbohydrates: 9g*
- *Protein: 2g*
- *Fat: 4g*
- *Saturated Fat: 0g*

- ▶ *Sodium: 74mg*
- ▶ *Potassium: 137mg*
- ▶ *Fiber: 3g*
- ▶ *Sugar: 5g*
- ▶ *Vitamin C: 0mg*
- ▶ *Calcium: 110mg*
- ▶ *Iron: 1mg*

Hemp Seed Nuggets

One of the best things about **hemp** seeds is that it is incredibly easy to incorporate them into your diet. Not only are these recipes easy to make, but you can be sure that you are **putting** only the healthiest ingredients on the table.

Prep time: 20 minutes Servings: Yield: 9 nuggets
(3 per serving)

Ingredients:

- ¾ cup (120g) hulled hemp seeds
- ½ cup (120 ml) vegetable broth
- 2 tablespoons (10g) nutritional yeast
- 1 tablespoon Savory Herb Mix (see Savory Herb Mix)
- ¼ teaspoon salt
- ¼ teaspoon ground black pepper
- 2 tablespoons (10g) psyllium husks
- 2 tablespoons (14g) unflavored pea protein powder or other unflavored vegan protein powder of choice

Directions:

▶ Preheat the oven to 350°F (177°C) and line a rimmed baking sheet with parchment paper

▶ In a blender or food processor, blend the hemp seeds, broth, Nutritions: al yeast, herb blend, salt, and pepper

▶ Transfer the mixture to a small bowl and stir in the psyllium husks and protein powder until the ingredients are thoroughly combined and a sticky dough forms

▶ Using wet hands, shape the dough into 9 nuggets, about 2 tablespoons (30g) each, and place on the baking sheet

▶ Bake for 20 minutes, flipping the nuggets over halfway through the baking time, until they are firm to the touch and slightly golden on the top and bottom

▶ Refrigerate for up to 3 days or freeze, tightly wrapped, for up to a month

▶ To reheat – Place in a preheated 300°F (150°C) oven for 5 minutes or until warmed through

Nutritions:

▶ *Calories: 278kcal*
▶ *Carbohydrates: 10g*
▶ *Protein: 18g*
▶ *Fat: 20g*
▶ *Saturated Fat: 2g*
▶ *Sodium: 692mg*
▶ *Potassium: 532mg*
▶ *Fiber: 5g*
▶ *Sugar: 1g*
▶ *Vitamin C: 81mg*
▶ *Calcium: 1mg*
▶ Iron: 4mg

Mixed Berry Mousse

Here's a good reason berry mousse recipes aren't that prevalent: Berries contain lots of juice, and that can ruin the texture of a delicate mousse, which should be creamy and rich. Plus, the fruit flavor produced by most recipes is too subtle.

Prep time: 10 minutes Servings: 6 servings

Ingredients:

- ▶ 20 oz thawed frozen blackberries (4 cups) blueberries, raspberries, /or strawberries
- ▶ 6 tbsp sugar divided
- ▶ 1 tsp finely grated lemon zest
- ▶ Pinch table salt
- ▶ 1 1/2 tsp unflavored vegan gelatin (agar agar)
- ▶ 1/2 cup coconut cream
- ▶ 3 oz vegan cream cheese softened

Directions:

- ▶ Combine berries, 3 tablespoons sugar, lemon zest, and salt in a bowl and let sit for 30 minutes, stirring occasionally.
- ▶ Strain berries through a fine-mesh strainer over a separate bowl; transfer berries to Ace blender and set aside. Transfer 3 tablespoons drained juice into a small bowl, sprinkle gelatin over the top, and let sit until gelatin softens about 5 minutes. Meanwhile, microwave remaining juice until reduced to 3 tablespoons, 4 to 5 minutes. Whisk gelatin mixture and remaining 3 tablespoons sugar into reduced juice until dissolved.
- ▶ Lock blender lid in place, then process berries on Medium speed until smooth, about 30 seconds. Add gelatin mixture, coconut cream, and vegan cream cheese to a blender, return lid, and process on medium speed until combined, about 10 seconds. Increase speed to high and process until smooth, about 30 seconds, pausing to scrape down sides of blender jar as needed.
- ▶ Portion mousse into 4 individual serving dishes. Cover with plastic wrap and refrigerate until set, at least 4 hours or up to 2 days. Serve.

Nutritions:

- ▶ *Calories: 245 kcal*
- ▶ *Carbohydrates: 42g*
- ▶ *Protein: 3g*
- ▶ *Fat: 9g*
- ▶ *Saturated Fat: 6g*
- ▶ *Sodium: 50mg*
- ▶ *Potassium: 186mg*
- ▶ *Fiber: 5g*
- ▶ *Sugar: 35g*
- ▶ *Vitamin C: 3mg*
- ▶ *Calcium: 44mg*
- ▶ *Iron: 2mg*

Almond Green Beans

This classic French recipe of green beans with almonds has been elevated with sautéed shallots, garlic, freshly grated lemon zest, and lemon juice. This elegant, simple, and delicious vegetable side dish comes together quickly and is great for the holidays!

Prep time: 10 minutes Servings: 6 servings

Ingredients:

- 1 lb (16 oz) French green beans haricot verts, trimmed
- 2 tablespoons unsalted vegan butter
- ¼ heaping cup raw sliced almonds
- 2 medium shallots finely diced
- 2 medium garlic cloves finely minced
- zest of one small lemon
- 2 teaspoons freshly squeezed lemon juice

- ▶ kosher salt to taste
- ▶ freshly ground black pepper to taste

Directions:

- ▶ Bring a large pot of water to a boil. Season the water liberally with kosher salt (it should be very salty to taste). Salting the cooking water aggressively accomplishes two tasks: it ensures that the green beans will be seasoned properly inside and out and helps them retain their bright green color after cooking. For make-ahead tips, please read the notes section at the bottom of this recipe thoroughly.
- ▶ Blanch the green beans for 4 to 5 minutes, stirring occasionally, or until they are crisp-tender and slightly squeaky between your teeth. It is important that the green beans be slightly undercooked as they will be transferred directly to the skillet and will continue cooking during this time.
- ▶ Meanwhile, in a large skillet, melt the butter over medium-low heat until lightly bubbling. Add the sliced almonds and sauté, frequently stirring, for 2 to 3 minutes or until they start to turn golden brown. Reduce the heat to low and add the chopped shallots and garlic. Sauté for an additional 1 to 2 minutes, frequently stirring, until fragrant and lightly caramelized.
- ▶ Using a large slotted spoon, tongs, or kitchen spider, transfer the blanched green beans from the boiling water directly to the skillet. Sauté briefly, gently tossing the green beans with the almond mixture until evenly combined and the green beans are tender. Add the lemon zest and lemon juice, toss once again, and season to taste with salt and freshly ground pepper. Serve immediately.

Nutritions:

- ▶ *Calories: 89kcal*
- ▶ *Carbohydrates: 8g*

- *Protein: 3g*
- *Fat: 5g*
- *Sodium: 595 mg*
- *Potassium: 159 mg*
- *Fiber: 3g*
- *Sugar: 2 g*
- *Vitamin C: 4 mg*
- *Calcium: 45 mg*
- Iron: 1.1mg

Motivational Tips On Preserving the Food and Reusing the Food

Re-think how you eat your vegetables. Vegetables or tofu are not boring, either bland or flavorless. Marinating and seasoning are keys to this cooking. Treat vegetables and other vegan ingredients as if you are cooking meat.

CHAPTER 10

DAY 7

Luscious Greens And Peas

Luscious Greens sounds like a fancy word, but peanuts, beans, and peas all fall into that category. And they have some really good features: Luscious Greens are affordable, easy to find, and great for digestion.

While not often considered a vegetable, Luscious Greens are still a healthy source of dietary fiber and can help cleanse your system. Luscious Greens can also "get waste and food moving steadily through your system."

Almond Butter Low-Carb Bread

A slice of this bread is super moreish, loaded with protein from the almond butter, which can help to stabilize blood super and build & repair the body. Flaxseeds and psyllium husks provide a good source of fiber in this bread recipe, with the flax supplying good fats and omega-3. Enjoyable to eat as a morning breakfast, a lunchtime feast, or dipped in soup.

Prep time: 15 minutes Servings: 8 servings

Ingredients:

- ▶ 1 Cup Almond Butter
- ▶ 1/4 Cup Brown Flaxseed (ground)
- ▶ 2 Tbsp Coconut Flour
- ▶ 3 Tbsp Psyllium Husks
- ▶ 1 Tsp Baking soda
- ▶ 1 Tsp Baking Powder
- ▶ 1/2 Tsp Sea Salt
- ▶ 8 Tsp of Ener-G Egg Replacer
- ▶ 3 Tbsp Coconut Oil (melted)

- 1 Tsp Maple Syrup
- 1 Tsp Apple Cider Vinegar

Optional toppings:

- Sprinkle of Chia Seeds
- Sprinkle of Sesame Seeds
- Sprinkle of Poppy Seeds

Directions:

- Preheat the oven to 175°C, 350°F, gas mark 4.
- Grease your bread tin or line with parchment.
- Mix together all the dry ingredients and set them aside.
- In another bowl, beat the egg replacer, vinegar, and maple syrup well. Then add in the almond butter and butter/oil and blend well again.
- Stir the wet ingredients into the dry ingredients until a smooth batter forms.
- Scoop the batter into the prepared bread tin and sprinkle the seeds on top.
- Bake for 35 minutes or until the middle springs back when lightly touched.
- Remove from the oven and allow to cool before eating.

Nutritions:

- *Calories: 513 kcal*
- *Carbohydrates: 15g*
- *Protein: 14g*
- *Fat: 48g*
- *Saturated Fat: 12g*
- *Sodium: 1012mg*
- *Potassium: 723mg*
- *Fiber: 10g*

► *Sugar: 5g*
► *Vitamin C: 0mg*
► *Calcium: 276mg*
► *Iron: 2.5mg*

Sauteed Quick Lunch Veggies

The good old veggie saute is often done wrong: it's super soggy or completely bland in flavor. Think of that pile of limp zucchini and carrots you might eat at a wedding buffet. So why don't we do a total makeover on the old veggie saute? These sauteed vegetables are beautifully colored, bursting with flavor and crisp-tender in texture. They're the perfect side dish you've never had.

Prep time: 10 minutes Servings: 4 servings

Ingredients:

- ▶ 1 tablespoon olive oil
- ▶ 1 teaspoon minced garlic
- ▶ 1/2 red bell pepper, chopped
- ▶ 1/2 yellow bell pepper, chopped
- ▶ 6 cremini mushrooms, chopped

- ▶ 4 broccoli florets, chopped
- ▶ 1/2 zucchini, chopped
- ▶ 1/2 yellow summer squash, chopped
- ▶ 1/2 teaspoon dried oregano
- ▶ 2 tablespoons soy sauce
- ▶ 2 tablespoons vegetable stock

Directions:

- ▶ In a large saute pan over medium-high heat, add the olive oil and heat. Add the garlic and saute, stirring, for 1 minute. Add all of the vegetables and cook until just starting to wilt about 2 minutes. Add the oregano, soy sauce, and chicken stock and stir well and cook just until vegetables are wilted for about 3 minutes. Remove from heat and serve.

Nutritions:

- ▶ *Calories: 66 kcal*
- ▶ *Carbohydrates: 6g*
- ▶ *Protein: 3g*
- ▶ *Fat: 4g*
- ▶ *Saturated Fat: 0.5g*
- ▶ *Sodium: 531mg*
- ▶ *Potassium: 355mg*
- ▶ *Fiber: 2g*
- ▶ *Sugar: 2g*
- ▶ *Vitamin C: 75mg*
- ▶ *Calcium: 38mg*
- ▶ *Iron: 1mg*

Almond Butter Fudge

This almond butter fudge is a fast no-bake dessert that's naturally sweetened. It has an incredibly buttery flavor... without using a drop of actual butter. It's a healthy dessert you can feel good about indulging in!

Prep time: 10 minutes Servings: 21 servings

Ingredients:

- ½ cup Almond Butter (125g)
- ½ cup Coconut Butter (120ml) Melted
- ¼ cup Maple Syrup (60ml) or Golden Syrup
- ½ tsp Vanilla Extract

Directions:

▶ Add the almond butter, melted coconut butter, maple syrup, and vanilla extract to a mixing bowl and mix in well.

▶ Transfer to a parchment-lined loaf pan and smooth down with the back of a spoon.

▶ Place into the freezer to set.

▶ Cut into squares and enjoy. Keep it stored in either the freezer or the fridge.

Nutritions:

▶ *Calories: 91 kcal*

▶ *Carbohydrates: 4g*

▶ *Protein: 1g*

▶ *Fat: 8g*

▶ *Saturated Fat: 5g*

▶ *Sodium: 14mg*

▶ *Potassium: 53mg*

▶ *Fiber: 0.6g*

▶ *Sugar: 2.6g*

▶ *Vitamin C: 0mg*

▶ *Calcium: 24mg*

▶ *Iron: 0mg*

Cauliflower Bake

If you are sick of mac and cheese or potatoes but still want a hearty side, then this is the perfect alternative for you. This Loaded Cauliflower Bake combines the creamy cheesiness of classic macaroni and cheese and the amazing fix-ins (hint BACON) from a twice-baked potato into one incredible casserole. You definitely want to cook the cauliflower a little first to not take forever in the oven. After about 30 minutes, you won't be able to stand it any longer.

Prep time: 15 minutes Servings: 8 servings

Ingredients:

- ▶ 2 small heads of cauliflower, cut into florets
- ▶ 2 tbsp. Vegan butter
- ▶ 3 cloves garlic, minced
- ▶ 3 tbsp. all-purpose flour

- 2 c. soy milk
- 2 oz. vegan cream cheese softened
- 1 1/2 c. Vegan shredded cheddar, divided
- Kosher salt
- Freshly ground black pepper
- 6 slices tempeh, cooked and crumbled
- 1/4 c. sliced green onions

Directions:

- Preheat oven to 350°. In a large pot of salted boiling water, blanch cauliflower, 3 minutes. Drain and squeeze cauliflower of water.
- Make the cheese sauce: In a large skillet, melt vegan butter. Add garlic and cook until fragrant, 1 minute, then add flour and stir until golden, 2 minutes. Add soy milk and bring to a low simmer, then add vegan cream cheese, whisking until combined. Remove from heat and stir in 1 cup vegan cheddar until melted, then season with salt and pepper.
- In a 9"-x-13" dish, add drained cauliflower. Pour over the cheese sauce and stir until combined. Stir in all but 1 tablespoon each cooked tempeh and green onions until combined, then top with remaining vegan cheddar, tempeh, and green onions.
- Bake until cauliflower is tender and cheese is melty, 30 minutes.

Nutritions:

- *Calories:175 kcal*
- *Carbohydrates: 11g*
- *Protein: 9g*
- *Fat: 10g*
- *Saturated Fat: 2g*
- *Sodium: 135mg*
- *Potassium: 353mg*
- *Fiber: 1g*

- ► *Sugar: 5g*
- ► *Vitamin C: 33mg*
- ► *Calcium: 228mg*
- ► *Iron: 1mg*

Motivational Tips On Preserving the Food and Reusing the Food

Veganize your favorites! Stick with what you know and just make it vegan. If you love sandwiches or scrambled eggs, then just make vegan versions of it.

CHAPTER 11

DAY 8

Around The World With Plants

The land use of livestock is so large because it takes around 100 times as much land to produce a kilocalorie of beef or lamb versus plant-based alternatives. The same is also true for protein – it takes almost 100 times as much land to produce a gram of protein from beef or lamb versus peas or tofu.

Coconut and Berries Smoothie

Just 3 ingredients are needed for this delicious Coconut Berry Smoothie! High in potassium, vitamin C, and electrolytes, this beautiful dairy-free smoothie is hydrating, and the perfect pick me up.

Prep time: 5 minutes Servings: 4 servings

Ingredients:

► 1 ½ cups frozen mixed berries or fresh if you prefer
► 1 cup pure coconut water
► 1 very ripe banana, large
► a few ice cubes if you are using fresh fruit

Directions:

► Add all ingredients to a high-speed blender.
► Blend until smooth, about 30 seconds.

Nutritions:

- ► *Calories:66 kcal*
- ► *Carbohydrates: 16g*
- ► *Protein: 1g*
- ► *Fat: 0.5g*
- ► *Saturated Fat: 0g*
- ► *Sodium: 64mg*
- ► *Potassium: 343mg*
- ► *Fiber: 3g*
- ► *Sugar: 9g*
- ► *Vitamin C: 21mg*
- ► *Calcium: 25mg*
- ► *Iron: 0.5mg*

Mexican Cauliflower Rice

With one pan and 25 minutes, low carb Mexican Cauliflower Rice can be on your table. This tasty side dish is the perfect addition to a festive Taco Tuesday spread and an easy way to squeeze just a little more Nutritions: onto your plate without sacrificing one bit of flavor! Naturally Whole30, paleo, grain-free, and keto-friendly.

Prep time: 10 minutes Servings: 4 servings

Ingredients:

- ► 1large head of cauliflower, riced
- ► 1 tbsp olive oil
- ► 1 medium white onion, finely diced
- ► 2 cloves garlic, minced
- ► 1 jalapeno, seeded and minced
- ► 3 tbsp tomato paste

- ► 1 tsp sea salt
- ► 1 tsp cumin
- ► ½ tsp paprika
- ► 3 tbsp fresh chopped cilantro
- ► 1 tbsp lime juice

Directions:

- ► Rice the cauliflower. Slice the florets from the head of the cauliflower. Fit a food processor with the s-blade. Place half the florets into the bowl of the food processor and pulse until riced, scraping down the sides once halfway through to catch any larger pieces. Scrape out the riced cauliflower and repeat with the remaining florets.
- ► Heat a skillet over medium-high heat. Add the oil and heat until it shimmers. Add the onion and sautee until soft and translucent, occasionally stirring, 5-6 minutes.
- ► Add the garlic and jalapeno and sautee until fragrant, 1-2 minutes.
- ► Add the tomato paste, salt, cumin, and paprika and stir into the vegetables.
- ► Add the cauliflower rice and stir continuously until all ingredients are incorporated. Continue sautéing, occasionally stirring, until the cauliflower releases its liquid and is dry and fluffy.
- ► Remove the Mexican cauliflower rice from heat. Stir in the cilantro and lime juice. Serve immediately.

Nutritions:

- ► *Calories: 110 kcal*
- ► *Carbohydrates: 17g*
- ► *Protein: 5g*
- ► *Fat: 4g*
- ► *Saturated Fat: 1g*
- ► *Sodium: 654mg*

- *Potassium: 829mg*
- *Fiber: 5.5g*
- *Sugar: 7g*
- *Vitamin C: 112mg*
- *Calcium: 67mg*
- *Iron: 2mg*

Broccoli Crispy Bread

This cheesy broccoli is baked in the oven but comes out super crispy! It can be eaten as finger food or appetizer with ranch dip or served as a healthy side dish with dinner or any meal. Kids and adults love it! It will soon be a family favorite.

Prep time: 10 minutes Servings: 8 servings

Ingredients:

- 2 large heads of broccoli (chopped into bite-size pieces)~ 900g
- 1 cup Italian bread crumbs
- 1 cup grated sharp vegan cheddar cheese
- 1/4 cup fresh grated vegan parmesan cheese (refrigerated)
- 4 Tbsp Ener-G Egg Replacer
- 1 tbsp soy milk
- 1 tsp garlic powder

Directions:

▶ Preheat your oven to 400 degrees and line a baking sheet with parchment paper.

▶ In a medium-size bowl, whisk the eggs replacer and milk together.

▶ In a separate bowl, mix the Italian bread crumbs, cheddar cheese, parmesan cheese, and garlic powder together.

▶ Dip each piece of broccoli in the "egg" mixture until well coated, and then dip them in the cheese and bread crumb mixture until completely covered. In order to get good coverage, I sprinkle them well and then really push the broccoli into the bread crumbs to get them to stick.

▶ Place the coated broccoli florets on your lined baking sheet, and bake for 18-25 minutes. It takes about 20 minutes in my oven, so just keep an eye on them! The baking time will partly depend on the size of your broccoli pieces.

▶ Enjoy immediately. They are delicious alone, but we like to dip them in ranch dressing.

Nutritions:

▶ *Calories: 173 kcal*

▶ *Carbohydrates: 18g*

▶ *Protein: 10g*

▶ *Fat: 7g*

▶ *Saturated Fat: 1g*

▶ *Sodium: 285mg*

▶ *Potassium: 416mg*

▶ *Fiber: 4g*

▶ *Sugar: 3g*

▶ *Vitamin C: 101mg*

▶ *Calcium: 225mg*

▶ *Iron: 2mg*

Bolognese Zucchini

When you cook zucchini low and slow for 4 hours, something magical happens — it turns into an ultra-creamy sauce, perfect for pasta. You can serve this "meaty" sauce on your favorite veggie noodles, gluten-free noodles, or even regular old pasta, and you'll be amazed at how tasty and simple it is.

If you want to cook this in a slow cooker, sauté the onions and sausage before adding them with the rest of the ingredients into the slow cooker. Program your Crockpot to cook on low for 6 to 8 hours or until the zucchini is super tender.

Prep time: 10 minutes Servings: 4 servings

Ingredients:

- ► 1 tbsp. olive oil
- ► 1 onion, chopped
- ► 5 medium zucchini, chopped

- 1/2 c. water
- 1 Vegan bouillon cube
- 3/4 lb. vegan pasta such as rigatoni
- juice of a half lemon
- 1 c. vegan grated Parmesan
- pinch red pepper flakes

Directions:

- In a large pot (or Dutch oven) over medium heat, heat olive oil. Add onion and cook until soft, about 6 minutes. Stir in zucchini, water, and bouillon cube. Season with salt and pepper.
- Reduce heat to low and cover the pot. Cook for 4 hours, often stirring, until the zucchini is falling apart. (It will be mushy, and that's good!)
- When the sauce is almost ready, bring a large pot of boiling salted water to a boil. Add rigatoni and cook according to package instructions. Drain.
- Season sauce with salt and pepper, then stir in lemon juice, Parmesan, and red pepper flakes. Serve immediately.

Nutritions:

- *Calories: 514 kcal*
- *Carbohydrates: 75g*
- *Protein: 21g*
- *Fat: 14g*
- *Saturated Fat: 2.5g*
- *Sodium: 353mg*
- *Potassium: 897mg*
- *Fiber: 6g*
- *Sugar: 10g*
- *Vitamin C: 51mg*

▶ *Calcium: 262mg*

▶ *Iron: 2mg*

Motivational Tips On Preserving the Food and Reusing the Food

Try not to go shopping when you are hungry. Before you head to the grocery, get a banana to satisfy any cravings. When you are hungry, you tend to make impractical choices like buying things you don't really need. Or just shop online!

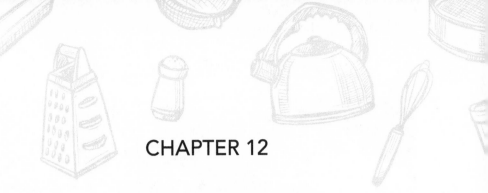

CHAPTER 12

DAY 9

Lively Grains And Greens

Most people grew up eating whole grains that are grown in the United States: wheat, corn, rice, and oats. But alternative or "ancient" grains are becoming more and more popular with people interested in adding more variety to their diets. With a distinctive taste and more flavor than most traditional grains, alternative grains are often a richer source of nutrients.

Pumpkin Bread

This moist & delicious pumpkin bread is the perfect cozy fall treat! Warmly spiced with nutmeg, allspice, and cinnamon, it's healthy and easy to make.

Prep time: 20 minutes Servings: 8 servings

Ingredients:

- ▶ Cooking spray for pan
- ▶ 2 c. all-purpose flour
- ▶ 1 tsp. ground cinnamon
- ▶ 1 tsp. baking soda
- ▶ 1/2 tsp. baking powder
- ▶ 1/2 tsp. kosher salt
- ▶ 1/4 tsp. ground ginger

- ▶ 1/4 tsp. ground nutmeg
- ▶ 1/2 c. (1 stick) vegan butter, melted
- ▶ 1 1/4 c. granulated sugar
- ▶ 1 c. pumpkin puree
- ▶ 1/4 c. vegan sour cream
- ▶ 3 tsp of Ener-G Egg Replacer
- ▶ 1 tsp. pure vanilla extract
- ▶ Cinnamon-sugar, for sprinkling (optional)

Directions:

- ▶ Preheat oven to 350°. Line an 8"-x-4" loaf pan with parchment paper, then grease with cooking spray (or softened butter).
- ▶ In a large bowl, whisk together flour, cinnamon, baking soda, baking powder, ginger, nutmeg, and salt.
- ▶ In a separate large bowl using a hand mixer, beat melted butter, sugar, pumpkin puree, vegan sour cream, Ener-G Egg Replacer and vanilla.
- ▶ Gradually add dry ingredients to wet ingredients until just combined. Transfer batter to the prepared pan, then sprinkles with cinnamon sugar if using.
- ▶ Bake until a toothpick inserted into the center of the loaf comes out clean, about 50 minutes to 1 hour.

Nutritions:

- ▶ *Calories: 174 kcal*
- ▶ *Carbohydrates: 5g*
- ▶ *Protein: 1g*
- ▶ *Fat: 17g*
- ▶ *Saturated Fat: 3.6g*
- ▶ *Sodium: 471mg*
- ▶ *Potassium: 113mg*
- ▶ *Fiber: 0g*

▶ *Sugar: 1g*
▶ *Vitamin C: 1mg*
▶ *Calcium: 24mg*
▶ Iron: 0mg

Herbed Spaghetti Squash

It's called spaghetti squash because the roasted flesh shreds into strands like spaghetti. Use it as a lower-carb and gluten-free replacement for spaghetti noodles in recipes.

Prep time: 5 minutes Servings: 4 servings

Ingredients:

- ► 1 small spaghetti squash, about 2 1/4 pounds
- ► 2 1/2 tablespoons butter
- ► 2 1/2 tablespoons finely chopped mixed soft herbs, such as basil, chives, chervil, parsley, and sage
- ► 1/2 teaspoon salt
- ► 1/8 teaspoon freshly ground black pepper

Directions:

▶ Preheat the oven to 375 degrees F.

▶ Using a sharp knife, cut the squash in half lengthwise and place, cut
side down, in a baking dish. Add enough water to come 1/2-inch up
the sides of the baking dish and cover with aluminum foil. Bake for
45 minutes until the squash is easily pierced with a paring knife. Turn
squash over and cover with foil again and continue to cook another
15 minutes until the squash is very tender. Remove from the oven,
uncover, and allow to cool slightly. Using a spoon, remove the seeds
and discard them. Using a fork, gently pull the strands of squash away
from the peel and place the squash strands into a mixing bowl.

▶ Heat a skillet. Add the butter, spaghetti squash, herbs, salt, and
pepper and toss thoroughly but gently to heat and combine. Serve
immediately or cover and keep warm until ready to serve.

Nutritions:

▶ *Calories: 87kcal*

▶ *Carbohydrates: 7g*

▶ *Protein: 4g*

▶ *Fat: 6g*

▶ *Saturated Fat: 0.5g*

▶ *Sodium: 295mg*

▶ *Potassium: 497mg*

▶ *Fiber: 3g*

▶ *Sugar: 4g*

▶ *Vitamin C: 28mg*

▶ *Calcium: 62mg*

▶ Iron: 1mg

Avocado Broccoli Soup

This Broccoli Avocado Soup recipe is comforting, delicious, and perfect for the entire family to enjoy.

It is so unfortunate, but children are exposed to processed foods all the time. What they really need instead is real healthy food, especially leafy green vegetables. Kids need to eat vegetables every day for optimal development. This recipe is just a great way to incorporate ingredients their bodies really need!

Prep time: 10 minutes Servings: 4 servings

Ingredients:

► 1 tablespoon olive oil, avocado oil, vegan butter,
► 1 medium sweet onion (roughly chopped)
► 3 garlic cloves (roughly chopped)
► 1 teaspoon sea salt
► ½ teaspoon black pepper

- 1½ lbs broccoli, cut into florets, stems peeled, and cut into rounds
- 6 cups chicken broth or vegetable broth (water also works)
- juice from ½ lemon
- 2 cups baby spinach, kale, Swiss chard, or other greens (roughly chopped)
- 1 cup fresh parsley, roughly chopped, stems removed
- 2 California Avocados, reserve ½ avocado for serving

Directions:

- Heat oil in a large saucepan over medium-high heat.
- Add onion and garlic; cook 5 minutes, or until onion is softened.
- Add broth and broccoli. Increase heat to high; bring to a boil.
- Reduce to low, cover, and simmer 5 minutes.
- Add avocados and simmer for 1 minute.
- Using an immersion blender, purée to desired consistency. Or, carefully transfer mixture to a stand blender and purée in batches.
- Season with salt and pepper. Divide between 4 bowls. Garnish with pistachios and kale chips. Serve immediately, refrigerating any leftovers.

Nutritions:

- *Calories: 287kcal*
- *Carbohydrates: 27g*
- *Protein: 9g*
- *Fat: 19g*
- *Saturated Fat: 2.7g*
- *Sodium: 1497mg*
- *Potassium: 1106mg*
- *Fiber: 13g*
- *Sugar: 8g*
- *Vitamin C: 76mg*
- *Calcium: 254mg*
- *Iron: 6mg*

Tempeh Curry Laksa

This dish serves 2 people; if you're a fan of Laska, you will love this recipe if you don't like tempeh swap with tofu.

Prep time: 10 minutes Servings: 4 servings

Ingredients:

- ▶ 700g of Pad Thai Noodles
- ▶ 250g of Tempeh
- ▶ 1 Tbps Curry powder
- ▶ 1 Fresh Red Chilli
- ▶ 1 Tin of Coconut milk
- ▶ 1 Carrot
- ▶ 1 Bunch Of Bok choy
- ▶ 1 Broccoli
- ▶ 1 Onion
- ▶ 2 Tbsp soy sauce/tamari

- ▶ 4 cups of Water
- ▶ 1 Tbsp Oil
- ▶ Salt & pepper

Directions:

- ▶ Heat a large saucepan with oil, finely dice an onion, red chili, and sauté, add soy sauce, curry powder followed by 1 tbsp of the coconut milk, stir for 3-5 minutes
- ▶ Stir slowly, season with salt & pepper, add the rest of the coconut milk. Add four cups of water, and leave on low heat to simmer for 20 minutes.
- ▶ Boil hot water, place noodles into a heat-proof bowl, cook for 4 minutes, do not overcook, drain and run under cold water to stop them cooking, then add into the laksa sauce.
- ▶ Heat oil in a pan, add Tempeh & fry until golden. Set aside.
- ▶ Dice carrot into thin sticks, and cut the broccolini into florets size. Add veg to the laska in the last 10 minutes. Then add bok choy within the last 2 minutes.
- ▶ Serve with the Tempeh on top

Nutritions:

- ▶ *Calories: 596 kcal*
- ▶ *Carbohydrates: 66g*
- ▶ *Protein: 25g*
- ▶ *Fat: 25g*
- ▶ *Saturated Fat: 15g*
- ▶ *Sodium: 875mg*
- ▶ *Potassium: 1339mg*
- ▶ *Fiber: 6g*
- ▶ *Sugar: 6g*
- ▶ *Vitamin C: 84mg*

- *Calcium: 317mg*
- Iron: 7mg

Motivational Tips On Preserving the Food and Reusing the Food

Buy frozen foods so you can store vegetables or fruits longer and just get what you need from the freezer. It's stable, and it won't rot as fast as when you stock fresh vegetables. You can also mix your shopping list with fresh and frozen if you want to.

CHAPTER 13

DAY 10

Satisfied With Herbs And Swiss

The herbs are used for the treatment of diseases, in cosmetics, or for aromatherapy, as well as for cooking, to enhance the flavor of the prepared food. The plants are used mostly as fresh and are added to the dishes in the last minutes of the cooking or after it is finished.

Hemp Seeds Porridge

Porridge. Porridge is great... if you eat oats. Heck, even if you eat quinoa or amaranth, the grain-free "seeds" of the porridge world, porridge can be your thing. But, porridge just isn't in the cards for many of us who can't digest grains AND have a challenging time with quinoa and amaranth.

Prep time: 5 minutes Servings: 4 servings

Ingredients:

For four serves:

- ▶ 60 g hemp seeds, also called hemp hearts
- ▶ 40 g chia seeds black, white or mixed
- ▶ 20 g erythritol, xylitol, or sweetener of choice
- ▶ 1 tsp vanilla extract
- ▶ 2 tsp cinnamon powder
- ▶ 160 g almond meal (or whole almonds, see step 1)
- ▶ 350-440 g liquid, i.e., unsweetened almond milk, coconut milk, or coconut cream and water, cream, and water, my favorite personally is 220g cream with 220g water) the range is so you can make it thicker or thinner depending on how you like it.

For single serves:

- ▶ 15 g hemp seeds, also called hemp hearts
- ▶ 10 g chia seeds black, white or mixed
- ▶ 1 tsp erythritol, xylitol, or sweetener of choice
- ▶ 1/4 tsp vanilla extract
- ▶ 1/2 tsp cinnamon powder
- ▶ 40 g almond meal (or whole almonds, see step 1)
- ▶ 90-110 g liquid, i.e., unsweetened almond milk, coconut milk, or coconut cream and water, cream and water, my favorite personally is 55g cream with 55g water), the range is so you can make it thicker or thinner depending on how you like it.

Directions:

There are many ways to prepare this recipe, one or more? Hot or cold?

1. Serves four and uses a mixer

- If using whole almonds, mill 10 seconds/speed 8 / mc on

- Place all ingredients into the mixer, cook 5 minutes / 80 degrees/ speed 1 / mc on

2. Serves one and uses microwave

- Alternatively, microwave single serves (see notes) for 2 minutes, then rest 2 minutes

3. Serves four and prepared as overnight oats

- Place all ingredients into a jar and refrigerate 1 hour or overnight, scoop out serves as desired

4. Serves one and prepared as overnight oats

- Prepare a jar of the mixture, then scoop out single serves (70g) into jars and add the liquid. Refrigerate for 1 hour or overnight.

- You can prepare 5 jars, so breakfast is ready every day; just grab a jar and top with your desired toppings.

- You can even microwave it (remove the lid, microwave 1 minute) at this point if you decide you want it warm!

Notes

- To prepare single serves, you can make up a jar of the dry ingredients, then scoop 70g dry porridge mix and add 110g liquid.

Nutritions:

- ▶ *Calories: 652 kcal*
- ▶ *Carbohydrates: 30g*
- ▶ *Protein: 14g*
- ▶ *Fat: 58g*
- ▶ *Saturated Fat: 32g*
- ▶ *Sodium: 9mg*
- ▶ *Potassium: 936mg*
- ▶ *Fiber: 12g*
- ▶ *Sugar: 9g*
- ▶ *Vitamin C: 5mg*
- ▶ *Calcium: 197mg*
- ▶ Iron: 5mg

Sauteed Brussel Sprouts with Almonds and Radicchio

Brussels sprouts are one of those vegetables that seem to split eaters into two camps; you either love them or can't stand them. We think these SAUTÉED BRUSSELS SPROUTS are going to change all that. This recipe is super easy to prepare, but it's all about the flavors that come from a simple sauté of choice ingredients. I could go on and on (and on!) but instead...

Prep time: 20 minutes Servings: 8 servings

Ingredients:

▶ 12 oz. brussels sprouts (about 20), ends trimmed, tough outer leaves removed

▶ 1/2 head radicchio, cored and cut in half

▶ 1/2 Fuji apple, cored and cubed

▶ 1 oz. toasted Marcona almonds, sliced

▶ 1/4 c. shredded cashew cheese

Vinaigrette:

- 1/4 c. extra-virgin olive oil
- 2 tbsp. water
- 2 tbsp. sherry or red wine vinegar
- 1 tsp. dijon mustard
- 1 tbsp. finely minced shallot
- 2 tsp. maple syrup
- 1/4 tsp. salt
- 1/4 tsp. black pepper

Directions:

- Whisk together all vinaigrette ingredients until well blended.
- Using a mandoline or food processor with a slicing disk, shave the sprouts and radicchio.
- Toss the sprouts and radicchio with the apple and dressing until evenly coated. Divide among plates, and top each with almonds and cheese.

Nutritions:

- *Calories: 123 kcal*
- *Carbohydrates: 8g*
- *Protein: 3g*
- *Fat: 10g*
- *Saturated Fat: 1g*
- *Sodium: 92mg*
- *Potassium: 230mg*
- *Fiber: 2g*
- *Sugar: 3g*
- *Vitamin C: 37mg*
- *Calcium: 33mg*
- *Iron: 1mg*

Blackberry Lemonade

Cool down on a long, hot day with a fun and fruity blackberry lemonade! This easy recipe is a fun way to use those freshly picked blackberries! There are only a few ingredients you need to make the best blackberry lemonade ever. And chances are, you will have them available already!

Prep time: 5 minutes Servings: 4 servings

Ingredients:

- ▶ ¾ cup white sugar
- ▶ 4½ cups water, divided

- 1 cup blackberries
- 2 tablespoons white sugar
- 1 cup freshly squeezed lemon juice
- ice cubes

Directions:

- Heat 3/4 cup sugar and 1/2 cup water in a small saucepan over medium heat. Cook and stir until sugar has dissolved about 2 minutes. Let cool.
- Place blackberries and the remaining 2 tablespoons of sugar in a blender. Blend until smooth.
- Combine simple syrup, blended blackberries, the remaining 4 cups of water, and lemon juice. Place a fine-mesh sieve over a pitcher and pour lemonade into the pitcher. Discard solids. Serve over ice.

Nutritions:

- *Calories: 198 kcal*
- *Carbohydrates: 51g*
- *Protein: 1g*
- *Fat: 0.3g*
- *Saturated Fat: 0g*
- *Sodium: 1mg*
- *Potassium: 122mg*
- *Fiber: 2g*
- *Sugar: 47g*
- *Vitamin C: 31mg*
- *Calcium: 15mg*
- Iron: 0mg

Deep-Fried Okra

Fried okra is a tasty treat. Just coat okra with beaten egg and then seasoned cornmeal, cornflour, or semolina to give it an extra crunch. You can fry the pods whole, but there's nothing wrong with cutting the okra into bite-size pieces first to fry up into popcorn-like snacks. In either case, serve them plain, or offer a spiced aioli for dipping.

Prep time: 15 minutes Servings: 4 servings

Ingredients:

- ▶ 1 pound okra
- ▶ 3 tsp of energy egg G replacer
- ▶ 2 tablespoons water
- ▶ 1 1/2 cups cornmeal
- ▶ 1/2 teaspoon fine sea salt, plus more for optional sprinkling
- ▶ 1/4 teaspoon freshly ground black pepper

- 1/4 teaspoon cayenne, optional
- Vegetable oil, for frying

Directions:

- Gather the ingredients.
- Trim the stem ends off the okra pods. Cut the pods into bite-size pieces, if you like. Set aside.
- In a large bowl, dissolve egg replacer and add 2 more tablespoons of water. Beat them well, so the mixture is of a uniform, watery consistency. Set aside.
- In a second large bowl, combine the cornmeal, salt, pepper, and optional cayenne. Set aside.
- In a large heavy pot, heat at least half an inch of oil from 350 F to 375 F. Measure the temperature with a thermometer. Or, test it by dipping a piece of bread or the handle of a wooden spoon into the oil—it should sizzle immediately and steadily. If it doesn't sizzle, it's not hot enough. If it bubbles up violently, it is too hot.
- While the oil heats, put the okra in the egg replacer and toss it to coat the pods thoroughly. Lift the okra out, letting as much excess egg drip off as possible (you can also simply strain it in a colander if you prefer).
- Working in batches of 4 or 5 pods, use one hand to put the egg-coated okra in the cornmeal and the other hand to toss it to coat it completely with the cornmeal mixture. Note that you're using one hand to touch the wet okra and one hand to touch the dry cornmeal.
- Put the coated okra on a plate or baking sheet. Repeat with remaining okra pods.
- Fry the coated okra in batches. The pods should be in a single layer, and they shouldn't touch. Fry each batch until the coating turns brown and crispy (and the okra is tender inside)

- Use tongs or a slotted spoon to transfer the cooked okra to a layer of paper towels to drain.
- Repeat with the remaining okra.
- Serve fried okra hot, sprinkled with additional salt, if you like.

Nutritions:

- *Calories: 286 kcal*
- *Carbohydrates: 55g*
- *Protein: 6g*
- *Fat: 5g*
- *Saturated Fat: 1g*
- *Sodium: 303mg*
- *Potassium: 428mg*
- *Fiber: 6g*
- *Sugar: 3g*
- *Vitamin C: 26mg*
- *Calcium: 96mg*
- *Iron: 1mg*

Motivational Tips On Preserving the Food and Reusing the Food

Buy foods that are in season. It minimizes the addition of oils because we want the flavor to come out. It maximizes the Nutritions: al value because it is grown and picked when it is supposed to.

CHAPTER 14

DAY 11

Batter Up With Grains

Many batters are made by combining dry flours with liquids such as water, milk, or eggs. Batters can also be made by soaking grains in water and grinding them wet. Often a leavening agent such as baking powder is included to aerate and fluff up the batter as it cooks, or the mixture may be naturally fermented for this purpose as well as to add flavor.

Flaxseeds and Chia Waffles

Waffles can often seem like a bit of a pain to do at home because of needing a waffle iron, but once you invest in one, you won't be sorry. These nutritious and wholesome Chia & Flax Seed Waffles are a great way to start the day and, once cooled, can easily be frozen and put into the toaster for later.

Prep time: 20 minutes Servings: 4 servings

Ingredients:

- 1 cup whole-wheat pastry flour / 120 grams
- ¾ cup spelt flour / 90 grams
- 1 tbsp baking powder (aluminum free) / 13.8 grams
- ½ tsp baking soda / 2.3 grams
- ¼ tsp salt / 2 pinches
- 2 tbsp chia seeds / 20 grams
- 2 tbsp flax meal (ground flax seed) / 13 grams
- 2 cups almond milk or any non-dairy milk / 480 ml
- 1 tsp apple cider vinegar / 5 ml
- 1 tsp vanilla extract
- 1/3 cup raisins (optional) not included in nutrition info

On top:

- 1/2 banana, chopped
- handful of organic blueberries
- handful of black sesame seeds
- agave nectar, to taste

Directions:

- Mix the almond milk and the vinegar and set aside to curdle. Then add vanilla.

► In a large bowl, mix the whole wheat and spelled flour with the baking powder, baking soda, and salt.

► To the almond milk, add the chia seeds and flax meal. Whisk together.

► Add the almond milk mixture to the dry ingredients and mix until everything's just moistened. If the mixture is too dry, add a little more almond milk.

► Cook in a waffle iron, per instructions.

► This recipe makes 8-10 waffles.

Nutritions:

► *Calories: 646 kcal*
► *Carbohydrates: 112g*
► *Protein: 18g*
► *Fat: 14g*
► *Saturated Fat: 1g*
► *Sodium: 1497mg*
► *Potassium: 611mg*
► *Fiber: 15g*
► *Sugar: 20g*
► *Vitamin C: 5mg*
► *Calcium: 976mg*
► Iron: 8mg

Asparagus Mash

This is a great side recipe in case you're bored with sweet potato mash or cauliflower mash and want something a bit lighter and more refreshing.

It's really easy to make, but you should blanch your asparagus shoots before pureeing it and saute the onions for a sweeter flavor. Blanching the asparagus and adding in the lemon juice will also give you bright green color and a fresher taste.

Prep time: 10 minutes Servings: 8 servings

Ingredients:

▶ 10 asparagus shoots, chopped and blanched (2 min)
▶ 1/4 onion, diced and cooked in coconut oil

- ▶ 2 Tablespoons coconut cream
- ▶ 2 Tablespoons fresh parsley
- ▶ 1 teaspoon lemon juice
- ▶ 1/2 teaspoon salt (or to taste)
- ▶ Dash of pepper (omit for AIP)

Directions:

- ▶ Dice the onions.
- ▶ Chop the asparagus up into small pieces so that they will be easy to puree. Place the asparagus pieces into a pot of boiling water for 2 minutes and drain immediately.
- ▶ Saute the diced onion in some coconut oil or avocado oil. Saute until the onion turns translucent.
- ▶ Chop the parsley roughly.
- ▶ Place all the ingredients (make sure to drain the asparagus well) into a blender.
- ▶ Blend really well until a creamy mash forms.

Nutritions:

- ▶ *Calories: 19 kcal*
- ▶ *Carbohydrates: 1.6g*
- ▶ *Protein: 0.8g*
- ▶ *Fat: 1g*
- ▶ *Saturated Fat: 1g*
- ▶ *Sodium: 147mg*
- ▶ *Potassium: 74mg*
- ▶ *Fiber: 1g*
- ▶ *Sugar: 0.6g*
- ▶ *Vitamin C: 3.3mg*
- ▶ *Calcium: 9mg*
- ▶ *Iron: 0.7mg*

Strawberry Truffles

These Strawberry Truffles are smooth and creamy with an intense strawberry flavor. Made with just 5 ingredients, these top-notch treats are perfect for Valentine's Day, your anniversary, or just whenever you want to show someone how special they are to you.

Prep time: 20 minutes Servings: 20 truffles

Ingredients:

- ▶ 2 bars (3 1/2 oz each) premium Vegan dark chocolate (cocoa content between 55 and 60% cocoa mass)
- ▶ 2 cups strawberries (preferably frozen and organic)
- ▶ 2 tablespoons Imperial Sugar Extra Fine Granulated Sugar
- ▶ 1 cup freeze-dried strawberries
- ▶ 14 ounces chocolate coating (wafers/candy melts)

Directions:

▶ Chop chocolate bars into small pieces and place them in a bowl large enough to hold all ingredients. Set aside.

▶ Puree defrosted berries until smooth. Measure 1/2 cup + 1 tablespoon strawberry puree (any extra can be added to sparkling water for a fruit-infused drink) and place puree in a saucepan with the sugar and bring to a boil. Remove from heat and pour into a bowl containing chopped chocolate. Stir using a whisk until all chocolate is melted.

▶ Chop freeze-dried strawberries into small pieces. Lots of strawberry powder will be created, and that is fine. Add all of it to the above mixture.

▶ Allow mixture to firm up for 3-4 hours or overnight or until firm enough to be scooped and hold its shape.

▶ Using a melon baller, scoop out strawberry ganache into round balls. The remaining ganache can be pressed and rolled by hand into balls. Set aside.

▶ Melt chocolate coating according to manufacturer's directions.

▶ Place some chocolate coating on the palm of your hand and roll a round ganache ball into it. Place on plastic-lined cookie sheet. Repeat until all is done. If chocolate coating becomes too firm and/or cold, reheat it. Roll truffles a second time into the chocolate coating.

▶ If desired, decorate truffles with a small piece of freeze-dried strawberries adhered to truffles using a small amount of coating.

▶ Keep truffles refrigerated.

Nutritions:

▶ *per truffel: Calories: 142 kcal*
▶ *Carbohydrates: 24g*
▶ *Protein: 1g*
▶ *Fat: 5g*

- *Saturated Fat: 2.5g*
- *Sodium: 17mg*
- *Potassium: 141mg*
- *Fiber: 2g*
- *Sugar: 18g*
- *Vitamin C: 8mg*
- *Calcium: 13mg*
- Iron: 2mg

Zucchini Alfredo

While plain olive oil and herbs are fine and a dollop of ricotta is even better, the ne plus ultra of pasta plus zucchini, in our household's humble opinion, is zucchini alfredo. Just like the classic recipe for spaghetti carbonara, the traditional method of making fettuccine alfredo doesn't involve cream at all.

The recipes are kissing cousins in that way—both rely on the heat of just-cooked pasta to turn cheese and other thickening ingredients into a luxurious sauce.

Prep time: 15 minutes Servings: 4 servings

Ingredients:

▶ 3 tablespoons unsalted Vegan butter, divided

▶ 1 pound (3 medium-sized) zucchini, spiralized

▶ 2 cloves garlic, minced

- ▶ 2 tablespoons all-purpose flour
- ▶ 1 1/2 cups 2% non dairy milk, or more, as needed
- ▶ 1/2 teaspoon dried thyme
- ▶ 1/2 teaspoon dried oregano
- ▶ 1/4 cup coconut crem
- ▶ 1/4 cup freshly grated Vegan Parmesan cheese
- ▶ Kosher salt and freshly ground black pepper, to taste
- ▶ 2 tablespoons chopped fresh parsley leaves

Directions:

- ▶ Melt 1 tablespoon Vegan butter in a saucepan over medium heat. Add zucchini and cook, occasionally stirring, until tender and heated through, about 3-5 minutes; set aside.
- ▶ Melt the remaining 2 tablespoons of Vegan butter in the saucepan. Add garlic, and cook, frequently stirring, until fragrant, about 1-2 minutes. Whisk in flour until lightly browned, about 1 minute.
- ▶ Gradually whisk in milk, thyme, and oregano. Cook, constantly whisking, until incorporated, about 1-2 minutes. Stir in half and a half and Parmesan until slightly thickened, about 1-2 minutes. If the mixture is too thick, add more milk as needed; season with salt and pepper to taste.
- ▶ Stir in zucchini and gently toss to combine.
- ▶ Serve immediately, garnished with parsley, if desired.

Nutritions:

- ▶ *Calories: 235 kcal*
- ▶ *Carbohydrates: 15g*
- ▶ *Protein: 10g*
- ▶ *Fat: 16g*
- ▶ *Saturated Fat: 6g*
- ▶ *Sodium: 104mg*

- ► *Potassium: 824mg*
- ► *Fiber: 3g*
- ► *Sugar: 5g*
- ► *Vitamin C: 42mg*
- ► *Calcium: 202mg*
- ► *Iron: 2mg*

Motivational Tips On Preserving the Food and Reusing the Food

Go for the reduced or sale items. Arrive at the supermarket early so you can get the best fresh items on sale before anyone else gets a go with that.

CHAPTER 15

DAY 12

Sweet And Salty Balance

Many food cravings are simply natural reactions to a diet that is not balanced in sweet and salty/bitter tastes. Your body craves both sweet and salt because sweets are expanding in nature, and salts are contracting in nature. If your body is too expansive or too contracting, your cells do not remain properly hydrated, and your body will be out of balance. This causes poor health and food cravings.

Poppy Seeds and Lemon Muffins

You are going to love the moist texture and the zesty flavor of these lemon poppy seed muffins. They are soft, sweet, tangy, and so lemony.

Prep time: 5 minutes Servings: 12 muffins

Ingredients:

For the Muffins:

- 2¼ cups all-purpose flour 313g
- 2 teaspoons baking powder 8g
- ¼ teaspoon baking soda 2g
- 2 tablespoons poppy seeds 23g
- 1 cup sugar 186g
- 2 tablespoons lemon zest 6g
- 1 cup Vegan greek yogurt 245g
- ⅓ cup non dairy milk 78mL
- ½ cup unsalted vegan butter melted (113g)
- 4 tsp of Egg replacer
- 1 tablespoon fresh lemon juice 15mL
- 1 teaspoon vanilla extract 5mL
- ¼ teaspoon kosher salt 2g

For the Glaze:

- 1 cup powdered sugar 113g
- 2 tablespoons fresh lemon juice 30mL

Directions:

- Preheat oven to 425F. Line a 12-cup muffin pan with paper liners.
- For muffins: In a large bowl, sift together flour, baking powder, and baking soda. Whisk in poppy seeds and salt.

► In another large bowl, combine sugar and lemon zest. Working with your hands, rub the zest into the sugar until fully combined. Add vegan yogurt, non dairy milk, melted vegan butter, eggs replacer , lemon juice, and vanilla. Whisk until smooth. Pour into the flour mixture and fold just until combined. (Batter will be thick.) Divide batter evenly among paper liners.

► Bake for 15 to 17 minutes or until tops are golden brown and a toothpick inserted in the center comes out with a few moist crumbs. Let muffins cool in pan for 10 minutes. Remove and finish cooling on a wire rack.

► For the glaze: Whisk together powdered sugar and lemon juice until smooth in a small bowl. Drizzle over cooled muffins.

Nutritions:

► *Calories: 185 kcal*
► *Carbohydrates: 40g*
► *Protein: 4g*
► *Fat: 1.5g*
► *Saturated Fat: 0g*
► *Sodium: 85mg*
► *Potassium: 132mg*
► *Fiber: 1g*
► *Sugar: 20g*
► *Vitamin C: 4mg*
► *Calcium: 104mg*
► *Iron: 1mg*

Smashed Bean Sandwiches

This vegetarian salad relies on white beans as the base. The beans become so creamy when smashed that only a touch of vegan mayonnaise is needed to bring it together, and celery seed and tangy lemon juice intensify the flavor. It's ultra-versatile: slather it on thick bread slices as a sandwich, mound it on top of salad greens, or spread it on a croissant for an impressive brunch. In the summer, we add chopped basil, chives, or tarragon for an herby kick. It's unassumingly tasty, and we make it for quick lunches or dinner in a pinch.

Prep time: 20 minutes Servings: 4 servings

Ingredients:

- ▶ 1 stalk celery
- ▶ 3 small green onions
- ▶ 1 15-ounce can navy or cannellini beans
- ▶ 1 tablespoon Vegan mayonnaise
- ▶ 2 tablespoons lemon juice (1/2 lemon)
- ▶ 3/4 teaspoon celery seed
- ▶ 1/8 teaspoon garlic powder

- 1/4 – 1/2 teaspoon kosher salt
- Freshly ground black pepper
- 4 slices bread, large or 2 croissants
- 2 radishes
- 2 large leaves lettuce

Directions:

- Thinly slice the celery and green onions. Drain and lightly rinse the navy beans.
- In a medium bowl, roughly smash the beans with a fork, leaving about a third of their whole. Stir in the celery, green onions, mayonnaise, lemon juice, celery seed, garlic powder, kosher salt, and several grinds of black pepper. Taste and continue adding kosher salt a few pinches at a time until the flavor pops but is not too salty; the exact amount of salt will vary based on the brand of beans.
- Toast the bread. Thinly slice the radishes. Place lettuce on one slice of bread then spread the bean salad. Top with sliced radishes and the remaining slice of bread.

Nutritions:

- *Calories: 243 kcal*
- *Carbohydrates: 44g*
- *Protein: 12g*
- *Fat: 2g*
- *Saturated Fat: 0g*
- *Sodium: 570mg*
- *Potassium: 539mg*
- *Fiber: 8g*
- *Sugar: 3g*
- *Vitamin C: 4mg*
- *Calcium: 132mg*
- *Iron: 4mg*

Broccoli Patties with Avocado

The only damper on my charred broccoli enthusiasm these days is that it is harder than one would think to find glowingly fresh broccoli at the organic stores around me. You can tell broccoli is fresh when the heads are firm, with tight florets that take some effort to separate. Yet more often than not, a quick pat on the heads stocked in the produce bin reveals soft heads with distracted florets.

Prep time: 20 minutes Servings: 4 servings

Ingredients:

- ▶ 1 large head broccoli, about 750 grams (1 2/3 pounds)
- ▶ Olive oil for cooking
- ▶ 2 good handfuls chopped fresh herbs: cilantro, chervil, chives, and flat-leaf parsley all good choices
- ▶ 1 rounded tablespoon tahini (sesame paste, available from natural food stores and Middle-Eastern markets)

- ► 1 tablespoon lemon juice
- ► 1 ripe avocado, diced
- ► Fine sea salt
- ► Freshly ground black pepper

Directions:

- ► Preheat the oven to 200°C (400° F).
- ► Cut the broccoli into even-sized florets. Peel off any tough part on the stem, cut it lengthwise into four long logs, and slice not too thinly.
- ► Put the broccoli on a rimmed baking sheet, drizzle generously with olive oil, sprinkle with 1/4 teaspoon salt, and toss well to coat (it works best if you just use your hands). Insert into the oven and roast for 30 minutes until charred at the edges.
- ► While the broccoli is roasting, prepare the dressing. Put the herbs, tahini, lemon juice, and 1/4 teaspoon salt in a medium bowl. Sauce ingredients

- ► Stir with a fork to combine, and add a little fresh water, teaspoon by teaspoon, stirring all the while until you get a creamy but not too thick dressing. Taste and adjust the seasoning. Mixed sauce

- ► When the broccoli is cooked, transfer to the bowl, add the avocado, and toss to combine. Taste and adjust the seasoning again.
- ► Sprinkle with black pepper and serve. This is great when freshly made, but it can also sit at room temperature for a little while or get packed for lunch and refrigerated.

Nutritions:

- ► *Calories: 175 kcal*
- ► *Carbohydrates: 11g*
- ► *Protein: 8g*

- *Fat: 14g*
- *Saturated Fat: 2g*
- *Sodium: 109mg*
- *Potassium: 637mg*
- *Fiber: 9g*
- *Sugar: 2g*
- *Vitamin C: 45mg*
- *Calcium: 226mg*
- *Iron: 5mg*

Scrambled Tofu with Guacamole

To give yourself a head start, this tofu scramble stores in the fridge for 3-4 days and can be reheated in a microwave.

Prep time: 10 minutes Servings: 5 servings

Ingredients:

- ▶ 1 pkg Sunrise Medium Firm Tofu (454g) dried and crumbled
- ▶ 2 tsp. extra virgin olive oil
- ▶ 1 medium tomato, cut into chunks
- ▶ 1 clove fresh garlic, finely chopped
- ▶ 1 red finger chili chopped
- ▶ 3 whole spring onions, chopped
- ▶ ½ tsp. turmeric
- ▶ 3 avocados, mashed
- ▶ 6 slices sprouted grain bread

- micro sprouts of your choice for garnish
- salt and pepper to taste

Directions:

- Remove tofu from package, wrap in 3-4 sheets paper towel, put on a large plate, and place a heavy pan or bowl on top to squeeze out any excess moisture. After 10 minutes, change the paper towel and repeat, drying out the tofu as much as possible.
- Using a fork, crumble tofu to resemble scrambled egg and set aside.
- In a large fry pan on medium heat, add oil, onions, tomatoes, chili, and garlic. Sautee until tender, then add crumbled tofu and toss gently. Add turmeric and salt, and pepper. Correct seasoning to taste.
- Place bread into a toaster and while you wait, mash up the avocados. Divide avocado between the four slices of toast, spreading evenly. Top with Spicy Tofu Scramble and sprinkle with your favorite micro sprouts before serving.

Nutritions:

- *Calories: 407 kcal*
- *Carbohydrates: 36g*
- *Protein: 16g*
- *Fat: 25g*
- *Saturated Fat: 4g*
- *Sodium: 238mg*
- *Potassium: 929mg*
- *Fiber: 13g*
- *Sugar: 6g*
- *Vitamin C: 39mg*
- *Calcium: 178mg*
- *Iron: 4mg*

Motivational Tips On Preserving the Food and Reusing the Food

Try not to buy or refrain from processed vegan products such as labeled "free-from" because these are way more expensive than the ones you can make for yourself.

CHAPTER 16

DAY 13

Protein Boosting With Leaves

Protein is an essential nutrient. The body needs it to build and repair tissues. Although animal foods are usually highest in protein, some plants also contain high amounts. The best plant-based sources of protein include tofu, chickpeas, and peanuts, which are classed as legumes. That said, some vegetables can offer a good protein boost per calorie.

Breakfast Smoothie Bowl

Rise and shine with a delicious Smoothie Bowl recipe! Smoothie bowls are a great breakfast idea that packs in nutrients, fruit, and veggies.

A smoothie bowl is a smoothie eaten from a bowl instead of consumed from a cup. The biggest difference between a smoothie and a smoothie bowl is that smoothie bowls have toppings such as granola, seeds, and dried fruit, whereas normal smoothies don't.

Prep time: 5 minutes Servings: 2 servings

Ingredients:

Green Smoothie

- ▶ 1 medium frozen avocado
- ▶ 1 cup packed spinach

- 1 cup sliced frozen banana (~1 medium banana)
- 1 tablespoon ground flax
- 1/4 cup frozen cauliflower florets
- 3 pitted Medjool dates
- 1.25 cups unsweetened almond milk (or more, to taste)
- Toppings: 2 tablespoons dried coconut flakes, 1/4 teaspoon, chia seeds, and 1/3 cup sliced strawberries

Nutritions:

- *Calories: 371 kcal*
- *Carbohydrates: 48g*
- *Protein: 6g*
- *Fat: 20g*
- *Saturated Fat: 4g*
- *Sodium: 135mg*
- *Potassium: 1067mg*
- *Fiber: 13g*
- *Sugar: 28g*
- *Vitamin C: 42mg*
- *Calcium: 349mg*
- *Iron: 3mg*

Strawberry Smoothie

Prep time: 5 minutes Servings: 2 servings

- ► 1.5 cups whole frozen strawberries
- ► 1/2 medium banana
- ► 1/2 cup Tofu yogurt
- ► 1 cup 100% orange juice (or more, to taste)
- ► Toppings: 1/4 cup granola, 1/4 cup sliced strawberries, and 1/4 cup sliced banana

Nutritions:

- ► *Calories: 231 kcal*
- ► *Carbohydrates: 50g*
- ► *Protein: 5g*
- ► *Fat: 3g*
- ► *Saturated Fat: 0.6g*
- ► *Sodium: 35mg*

- ▶ *Potassium: 721mg*
- ▶ *Fiber: 5g*
- ▶ *Sugar: 26g*
- ▶ *Vitamin C: 154mg*
- ▶ *Calcium: 120mg*
- ▶ *Iron: 2mg*

Peanut Butter Banana Smoothie

Prep time: 5 minutes Servings: 2 servings

- ▶ 2 cups frozen sliced bananas (~2 medium bananas)
- ▶ 1/2 cup Tofu yogurt
- ▶ 1/2 tablespoon ground flax seeds
- ▶ 1 teaspoon vanilla extract
- ▶ 2 tablespoons all-natural peanut butter
- ▶ 1 cup unsweetened almond milk (or more, to taste)
- ▶ Toppings: 1/3 cup sliced banana, 1 tablespoon vegan mini chocolate chips, and 1 tablespoon peanut butter

Directions:

▶ Place all ingredients for your chosen smoothie bowl flavor in a high-speed blender. Start with half the amount of liquid and go up from there depending on how thick you like your smoothies.

▶ Blend on high for 1-2 minutes, stopping to scrape the sides as needed. Add more liquid to thin your smoothie bowl out.

▶ Transfer smoothie into 2 bowls and top with favorite toppings.

Nutritions:

▶ *Calories: 416 kcal*

▶ *Carbohydrates: 65g*

▶ *Protein: 13g*

▶ *Fat: 14g*

▶ *Saturated Fat: 2g*

▶ *Sodium: 240mg*

▶ *Potassium: 967mg*

▶ *Fiber: 6g*

▶ *Sugar: 31g*

▶ *Vitamin C: 15mg*

▶ *Calcium: 197mg*

▶ Iron: 2mg

Citrusy Brussel Sprouts

Brussels sprouts mellows their spicy flavor. Select Brussels sprouts that are about the same size, so they roast evenly. Citrus Roasted Brussels Sprouts are a delicious side for the holidays! This zesty 4-ingredient recipe is ready in about 30 minutes!

When people say they don't like Brussels sprouts, they just haven't had roasted Brussels sprouts. These Citrus Roasted Brussels Sprouts are delicious and nutritious, oven-roasted in oil and orange juice with a little orange zest for a twist on the traditional side dish.

Ingredients:

Prep time: 20 minutes Servings: 6 servings

- ▶ 2 pounds Brussels sprouts
- ▶ 2 tablespoons olive oil
- ▶ 2 oranges zested and juiced

- 1 teaspoon salt
- 1 teaspoon pepper

Directions:

- Preheat the oven to 425 degrees F.
- Wash Brussels sprouts and pat dry. Cut off the bottoms, and then cut each sprout into quarters.
- Place Brussels sprouts into a 9-inch x 9-inch baking dish.
- Add olive oil, 1 tablespoon orange zest, juice from both oranges, salt, and pepper to the sprouts. Mix to coat.
- Place in oven and roast for 10 minutes. Carefully stir and return to the oven to roast for 10 more minutes.
- Remove from oven when sprouts are fork-tender. Serve warm. Garnish with extra orange zest if desired.

Nutritions:

- *Calories: 129 kcal*
- *Carbohydrates: 19g*
- *Protein: 6g*
- *Fat: 5g*
- *Saturated Fat: 1g*
- *Sodium: 426mg*
- *Potassium: 672mg*
- *Fiber: 7g*
- *Sugar: 7g*
- *Vitamin C: 156mg*
- *Calcium: 86mg*
- *Iron: 2mg*

Roasted Almond Broccoli

This makes a great side dish with roasted or grilled tofu. It can also be turned into an easy salad — just toss it through a rocket with a little shredded cooked chicken.

Prep time: 10 minutes Servings: 4 servings

Ingredients:

- ► 1¼ pounds fresh broccoli crowns (about 3)
- ► Cooking spray
- ► 1 tablespoon olive oil
- ► 1 garlic clove, pressed
- ► ¼ teaspoon salt
- ► ¼ teaspoon black pepper
- ► 3 tablespoons sliced almonds

Directions:

- Preheat oven to 475°.
- Cut broccoli into 3-inch-long spears; cut thick stems in half lengthwise. Place broccoli in a single layer on a jelly-roll pan coated with cooking spray.
- Combine olive oil and garlic; drizzle broccoli with oil mixture, and toss well. Sprinkle with salt and pepper—Bake at 475° for 14 minutes (do not stir).
- While broccoli roasts, cook almonds, constantly stirring, in a small skillet over medium heat for 2 minutes or until toasted. Sprinkle roasted broccoli with toasted almonds.

Nutritions:

- *Calories: 139 kcal*
- *Carbohydrates: 7g*
- *Protein: 7g*
- *Fat: 11g*
- *Saturated Fat: 1g*
- *Sodium: 192mg*
- *Potassium: 367mg*
- *Fiber: 5g*
- *Sugar: 1g*
- *Vitamin C: 29mg*
- *Calcium: 186mg*
- *Iron: 3.5mg*

Asian Cucumber Salad

This easy Asian Cucumber Salad is made with crunchy cucumber, onion, rice wine vinegar, and a few secret ingredients! An easy Cucumber Salad that takes only 10 minutes to make and is guaranteed to be a hit.

Prep time: 15 minutes Servings: 4 servings

Ingredients:

- ▶ 4 cups of very thinly sliced seedless cucumbers (I used mini cucumbers)
- ▶ 1/4 cup of finely sliced red onion
- ▶ 1/4 cup of fined diced red pepper
- ▶ 1/4 cup of rice wine vinegar
- ▶ 1 teaspoon of maple syrup
- ▶ 1 teaspoon of sesame seeds
- ▶ 1/2 teaspoon toasted sesame oil

- 1/4 teaspoon of red pepper flakes
- 1/4 teaspoon of sea salt

Directions:

- Add a thinly sliced cucumber, red onion, diced red pepper, and sesame seeds to a medium-sized bowl. Set aside.
- In a small bowl, mix together rice wine vinegar, maple syrup toasted sesame oil, red pepper flakes, and sea salt.
- Add dressing to the cucumber bowl. Toss to mix everything.
- Serve immediately or cover and let sit in the refrigerator for an hour or two to let all the flavors meld.

Nutritions:

- *Calories: 36kcal*
- *Carbohydrates: 5g*
- *Protein: 1g*
- *Fat: 1g*
- *Saturated Fat: 0g*
- *Sodium: 150mg*
- *Potassium: 204mg*
- *Fiber: 1g*
- *Sugar: 3g*
- *Vitamin C: 12mg*
- *Calcium: 22mg*
- Iron: 0.4mg

Motivational Tips On Preserving the Food and Reusing the Food

Buy in bulk. You're going to consume it anyway. Also, if your meals are planned, you have an idea of what you will need ahead of time.

CHAPTER 17

DAY 14

Quick And Easy Wraps And Fry

Sometimes a little knowledge is a dangerous thing. Do you know why there is no ice cream in my home? Because if it's there, I'll eat it all. Chips and crackers? Are Quick and Easy Wraps and Fry.

Cinnamon Hemp Seeds "Oatmeal."

This recipe produces a nutty-tasting (as hemp seeds taste like sunflower seeds) version of apple-cinnamon oatmeal, and it will help anyone who is on a diet or looking for a nutritious meal. You can buy the seeds over the Internet or at many health food stores. There are no known allergy problems associated with the seeds.

Prep time: 5 minutes Servings: 2 servings

Ingredients:

- 1 cup water
- 1 cup apple cider
- 1 cup rolled oats
- 1 Granny Smith apple, diced
- 1 teaspoon ground cinnamon
- ½ teaspoon vanilla extract
- ¼ cup hemp milk
- ¼ cup hemp seeds

Directions:

- Bring water and apple cider to a boil in a medium saucepan. Stir in oats, reduce heat to low, and cook, occasionally stirring, for 3 minutes. Add apple, cinnamon, and vanilla extract. Cook, stirring gently, until tender, about 3 minutes more.
- Remove oatmeal from heat; add hemp milk and hemp seeds. Stir and serve.

Nutritions:

- *Calories: 393 kcal*
- *Carbohydrates: 67g*
- *Protein: 14g*

- ► *Fat: 6g*
- ► *Saturated Fat: 1g*
- ► *Sodium: 102mg*
- ► *Potassium: 580mg*
- ► *Fiber: 10g*
- ► *Sugar: 10g*
- ► *Vitamin C: 5mg*
- ► *Calcium: 103mg*
- ► Iron: 5mg

Creamy Squash Soup

This simple and creamy squash soup has just 6 ingredients, including squash, onion, olive oil, milk, and toasted walnuts. It is delicious when had with cream, maple roasted walnuts,. Fall in a bowl, very filling.

Prep time: 10 minutes Servings: 4 servings

Ingredients:

- ► 1 medium kabocha squash
- ► 1 yellow onion, roughly chopped
- ► 2 cloves garlic, smashed (optional – I like it both ways)
- ► 2 tablespoons olive oil
- ► 1 1/4 cup non dairy milk
- ► 1/4 teaspoon cayenne pepper
- ► toasted walnuts (2 oz or 28 halves)

- salt to taste
- 1 Tbsp coconut cream or to taste

Directions:

- Cut the squash into wedges. Scoop out the seeds, cut off the rind, and dice the squash.
- Heat the oil in a large skillet over medium-high heat. Add the squash, onion, and garlic. Sprinkle with a little salt and saute until lightly browned and the squash is cooked through.
- Place the cooked squash in a blender and add the milk and cayenne. Blend for 3-5 minutes or until the mixture is very smooth. Season generously with salt. Top each serving with toasted walnuts, and a teaspoon of coconut cream.

Nutritions:

- *Calories: 217 kcal*
- *Carbohydrates: 20g*
- *Protein: 5g*
- *Fat: 15g*
- *Saturated Fat: 2.5g*
- *Sodium: 47mg*
- *Potassium: 612mg*
- *Fiber: 3g*
- *Sugar: 6g*
- *Vitamin C: 15mg*
- *Calcium: 122mg*
- Iron: 1.5mg

Spicy Broccoli

Roast fresh broccoli with olive oil, salt, and crushed red pepper for a deliciously quick side dish! This Spicy Roasted Broccoli is incredible. Each floret is crispy on the outside but still tender.

Prep time: 5 minutes Servings: 4 servings

Ingredients:

- 12 oz fresh broccoli florets
- 3 – 4 tablespoons olive oil, extra virgin
- 1/4 tsp salt
- 1/2 tsp crushed red pepper flakes

Directions:

- Preheat oven to 425 degrees.
- Slice any large broccoli florets in half. Leave smaller ones whole.

▶ Spread florets in a single even layer on a baking sheet. Drizzle with olive oil. Sprinkle with salt and crushed red pepper flakes.

▶ Bake for 15 to 20 minutes. Florets should be soft with browning on the side that touches the pan.

▶ Remove from the oven and serve immediately!

Nutritions:

▶ *Calories: 124kcal*
▶ *Carbohydrates: 3g*
▶ *Protein: 3g*
▶ *Fat: 13g*
▶ *Saturated Fat: 1.5g*
▶ *Sodium: 174mg*
▶ *Potassium: 171mg*
▶ *Fiber: 2g*
▶ *Sugar: 0.5g*
▶ *Vitamin c: 17mg*
▶ *Calcium: 92mg*
▶ *Iron: 2mg*

Cauli Asparagus Soup

This delicious bowl of soup, despite being dairy-free, looks and feels pretty creamy. We have cauliflower to thank for that. The soup looks like a classic cream of asparagus, and your eyes will fool your palate to a certain extent. In addition to giving it a nice color, the bumpy superfood cauliflower provides a smoother texture to the soup than the less-starchy asparagus could achieve alone.

Prep time: 10 minutes Servings: 8 servings

Ingredients:

- ► 2 tablespoons olive oil
- ► 3 cloves garlic, chopped
- ► 6 cups vegetable broth
- ► 1 head cauliflower, broken into florets
- ► cayenne pepper, or to taste
- ► salt and ground black pepper to taste
- ► 2 pounds fresh asparagus, trimmed and chopped
- ► 2 tablespoons nasturtium petals, or more to taste
- ► 2 tablespoons diced asparagus tips, or more to taste

Directions:

- ► Heat olive oil in a large pot over medium heat. Cook and stir garlic in hot oil until fragrant, about 1 minute. Stir vegetable broth, cauliflower, cayenne pepper, salt, and black pepper into garlic. Bring to a simmer, reduce heat to medium-low, and cook until cauliflower is tender for about 15 minutes.
- ► Stir 2 pounds asparagus into cauliflower mixture and increase heat to high. Cook until asparagus is tender but still bright green, 5 to 6 minutes.
- ► Blend soup with an immersion blender until smooth; season with salt and black pepper. Ladle soup into bowls and garnish with flower petals and diced asparagus tips.

Notes: **You can add chopped onions, leeks, or shallots and saute them with the garlic.**

Use more or less broth or water to adjust the soup to your desired thickness.

▶ You can also blend this soup with a blender. Pour soup into a blender no more than half full. Cover and hold lid down; pulse a few times before leaving on to blend. Puree in batches until smooth.

Nutritions:

▶ *Calories: 90*
▶ *Fat: 4g*
▶ *Saturated Fat: 0.5g*
▶ *Sodium: 788mg*
▶ *Potassium: 557mg*
▶ *Carbohydrates: 13g*
▶ *Fiber: 5g*
▶ *Sugar: 6g*
▶ *Protein: 5g*
▶ *Vitamin C: 58 mg*
▶ *Calcium: 53mg*
▶ *Iron: 3 mg*

Motivational Tips On Preserving the Food and Reusing the Food

▶ *Cornstarch and arrowroot powder are good choices for making a sauce creamy and thick. The ratio of starch to water would always be 1:2. So for every 1 tablespoon of starch*
2 tablespoons of water should be added. This is both applicable to sweet and spicy dishes.

CHAPTER 18

DAY 15

Boost Your Energy With Zucchini And Carrot

Zucchini, also known as courgette, is a summer squash in the Cucurbitaceae plant family, alongside melons, spaghetti squash, and cucumbers. It can grow to more than 3.2 feet (1 meter) in length but is usually harvested when still immature — typically measuring under 8 inches (20 cm).

Although zucchini is often considered a vegetable, it is botanically classified as a fruit. It occurs in several varieties, which range in color from deep yellow to dark green. Both carrots and zucchini are good sources of vitamin B6 which can be used to boost your energy.

Coconut Yogurt

Coconut Yogurt is a great dairy-free plant-based alternative. Gluten-free, vegan, and low carb, this yogurt only uses 2 ingredients! This delicious, super simple homemade coconut yogurt recipe is made with just 3 ingredients and yields a perfectly thick and tangy dairy-free yogurt!

Prep time: 5 minutes Servings: 4 servings

Ingredients:

▶ 2 cups full fat coconut milk
▶ 1 Tbsp corn starch
▶ 1 tsp powder yogurt starter OR 2 tbsp store-bought unsweetened coconut yogurt

Directions:

▶ To begin making the coconut yogurt, start by setting aside 1tbsp of coconut milk to mix the yogurt starter into.

- ▶ Meanwhile, heat up the coconut milk and cornstarch together over medium heat, till the mixture reaches 82ºC, stirring occasionally.
- ▶ Leave the milk to cool down till between 42-44ºC and then add in the 1 tsp yogurt starter and coconut milk combination into the heated coconut milk and mix well. -OR- If you are using store-bought coconut yogurt, just add it to the heated coconut milk and stir well.
- ▶ This coconut yogurt mixture now needs to be 'incubated'** at around 44ºC for around 10-12 hours minimum. You can even leave it for up to 16 hours for a thicker, more tart yogurt.
- ▶ You can then store your coconut yogurt in a sterilized glass jar in the fridge. This usually lasts between 5-7 days.

Nutritions:

- ▶ *Calories: 287kcal*
- ▶ *Carbohydrates: 9g*
- ▶ *Protein: 3g*
- ▶ *Fat: 28g*
- ▶ *Saturated Fat: 25g*
- ▶ *Sodium: 19mg*
- ▶ *Potassium: 324mg*
- ▶ *Fiber: 3g*
- ▶ *Sugar: 4g*
- ▶ *Vitamin C: 4mg*
- ▶ *Calcium: 21mg*
- ▶ *Iron: 2mg*

Kelp Noodle Pad Thai

This recipe is thanks to Low Carb Emporium. They stock everything that is hard to find, kelp noodles, pili nuts, flax crackers, green lead stevia, monk fruit, and erythritol.

Prep time: 15 minutes Servings: 2–3 servings

Ingredients:

- ► 1 tbsp coconut oil
- ► 1 red onion
- ► 1 pack kelp noodles
- ► 2–3 heads bok choy, sliced in half lengthways, and washed
- ► 2 carrots, spiralized or finely chopped
- ► 3 tbsp activated pili nuts
- ► ½ bunch mint, chopped
- ► ½ bunch coriander, chopped
- ► Sauce
- ► 3 tbsp almond butter
- ► 1 lime, juiced
- ► 2 tbsp tamari
- ► 2 tbsp water2 cloves garlic
- ► 4 spring onions, chopped
- ► ½ chili, fresh, chopped (optional)

Directions:

- ► Prepare the noodles by plunging in a large bowl of room temperature water. Leave to sit while you prepare the rest of the recipe.
- ► To make the sauce, combine all ingredients in a small blender or food processor. Set aside.
- ► Heat coconut oil in a pan and sauté red onion until fragrant and translucent. Pour in the sauce and leave to cook until fragrant and beginning to caramelize about 2 mins.
- ► Drain the noodles and rinse. Add into the pan and toss until heated through and coated in the sauce. Transfer to plates.
- ► Place the bok choy, cut side down onto the pan to brown slightly,

about 2 minutes. Add to the plates with the spiralized or finely chopped carrot. Top with pili nuts, coriander, and mint.

Nutritions:

- *Calories: 406kcal*
- *Carbohydrates: 42g*
- *Protein: 14g*
- *Fat: 24g*
- *Saturated Fat: 8g*
- *Sodium: 1568mg*
- *Potassium: 1106mg*
- *Fiber: 10g*
- *Sugar: 11g*
- *Vitamin C: 96mg*
- *Calcium: 548mg*
- *Iron: 8mg*

Black Bean Brownies

It seems ludicrous to make your favorite recipes just once, but sometimes you don't have time for repeats when you're a food blogger! That catch... black beans. In addition to being gluten-free, a cup of black beans has about half the calories that a cup of all-purpose flour has, it's got 20% of your daily iron, AND it has a slightly higher protein content (15g). Brownies make you strong like bull.

Prep time: 10 minutes Servings: 16 servings

Ingredients:

► 1 (15.5 ounces) can black beans, rinsed and drained
► 4.5 tsp egg replacer powder
► 3 tablespoons vegetable oil
► ¼ cup cocoa powder
► 1 pinch salt
► 1 teaspoon vanilla extract
► ¾ cup white sugar
► 1 teaspoon instant coffee (optional)

Directions:

▶ Preheat oven to 350 degrees F (175 degrees C). Lightly grease an 8x8 square baking dish.

▶ Combine the black beans, eggs replacer powder, oil, cocoa powder, salt, vanilla extract, sugar, and instant coffee in a blender; blend until smooth; pour the mixture into the prepared baking dish.

▶ Bake in the preheated oven until the top is dry and the edges start to pull away from the sides of the pan, about 30 minutes.

▶ Nutritions: *Calories: 115kcal*

▶ *Carbohydrates: 17g*

▶ *Protein: 5g*

▶ *Fat: 3g*

▶ *Saturated Fat: 0.8g*

▶ *Sodium: 39mg*

▶ *Potassium: 160mg*

▶ *Fiber: 3g*

▶ *Sugar: 10g*

▶ *Vitamin C: 0mg*

▶ *Calcium: 21mg*

▶ *Iron: 1mg*

Brussel Sprouts Salad

If you are looking for the perfect salad to serve at your Thanksgiving or Christmas dinner, you are in luck because this simple Brussels Sprouts Salad is always a holiday favorite! The flavors are incredible, it is pretty to serve, and it holds up well, so you can make it in advance. Plus, our friends and family love it! It's a winning salad!

Prep time: 15 minutes Servings: 8 servings

Ingredients:

For the Dressing:

- ▶ 1/3 cup olive oil
- ▶ 1 tablespoon fresh lemon juice
- ▶ 2 tablespoons apple cider vinegar
- ▶ 1 tablespoon pure maple syrup
- ▶ 2 teaspoons Dijon mustard

- 1 clove garlic minced
- Kosher salt and black pepper to taste

For the Salad:

- 1 lb Brussels sprouts ends trimmed
- 1 large Honeycrisp apple chopped (or 2 small apples)
- 1/2 cup dried cranberries
- 1/2 cup sunflower seeds
- 1/3 cup shredded vegan Parmesan cheese
- Kosher salt and black pepper to taste

Directions:

- First, make the maple mustard dressing. Whisk together the olive oil, lemon juice, apple cider vinegar, pure maple syrup, mustard, and garlic in a small bowl or jar. Season with salt and pepper and set aside.
- Next, shave the brussels sprouts. Use a food processor with the slicing attachment and pulse until the brussels sprouts are thinly sliced. You can also use a mandoline or sharp knife if you don't have a food processor.
- Place the shredded brussels sprouts in a large bowl. Add the chopped apple, dried cranberries, sunflower seeds, and vegan Parmesan cheese. Drizzle the salad with the dressing and toss well. Season with salt and pepper and serve.

Nutritions:

- *Calories: 213kcal*
- *Carbohydrates: 17g*
- *Protein: 5g*
- *Fat: 15g*
- *Saturated Fat: 2g*
- *Sodium: 80mg*

- ► *Potassium: 317mg*
- ► *Fiber: 4g*
- ► *Sugar: 10g*
- ► *Vitamin C: 50mg*
- ► *Calcium: 68mg*

Iron: 1mg

Motivational Tips On Preserving the Food and Reusing the Food

If you need eggs in a recipe, you can make use of a flax egg. Combine one tablespoon of ground flaxseed meal with 3 tablespoons of water.

CHAPTER 19

DAY 16

An Easy Day With Strawberries And Cauliflower

This summer, strawberry and cauliflower salad is the dream. It's so perfect for a summer's day lunch and is super easy to prepare.

Crispy Cinnamon Squares

This classic, crispy treat with a twist of cinnamon is made easy by substituting Cinnamon Sugar Butter Spread for regular butter.

Prep time: 10 minutes Servings: 12 squares

Ingredients:

- 2 tablespoons unsalted vegan butter, plus more for the pan
- 1 10-ounce package marshmallows - Yummallo Vegan Marshmallows
- 6 cups cornflakes (Ralston)
- ¼ teaspoon ground cinnamon

Directions:

- Butter an 8-inch square baking pan and line with parchment, leaving an overhang on two sides.
- In a large saucepan, cook the butter and marshmallows over medium heat, stirring until melted. Mix in the cornflakes and cinnamon.
- Press the cornflake mixture evenly into the prepared pan. Let cool completely, then lift out and cut into squares.

Nutritions:

- *Calories: 134kcal*
- *Carbohydrates: 30g*
- *Protein: 2g*
- *Fat: 2g*
- *Saturated Fat: 1g*
- *Sodium: 112mg*
- *Potassium: 37mg*
- *Fiber: 1g*
- *Sugar: 14g*
- *Vitamin C: 9mg*
- *Calcium: 2mg*
- *Iron: 3mg*

Asian Green Beans and Walnut Butter

These Asian Green Beans are packed with spicy flavor from chili garlic sauce, ginger. Walnuts add toasty flavor and texture. This is an easy way to change up a vegetable serving that just about nobody can turn down.

Make-Ahead: If you make your own walnut butter, you'll have some leftovers; they can be refrigerated in an airtight container for up to 3 months.

Prep time: 10 minutes Servings: 4 servings

Ingredients:

- ▶ 1 1/2 pounds green beans, trimmed
- ▶ 2 tablespoons walnut butter
- ▶ 2 tablespoons wheat-free tamari
- ▶ 2 teaspoons toasted sesame oil

- ▶ 1 tablespoon mirin (rice wine; may substitute water)
- ▶ 1/2 teaspoon sugar
- ▶ 1 tablespoon vegetable oil
- ▶ 1 large clove garlic, minced
- ▶ 1 teaspoon finely chopped fresh ginger
- ▶ 1/2 teaspoon crushed red pepper flakes or more as needed

Directions:

- ▶ Heat a few inches of water in a saucepan with a steamer basket over medium heat. Place the green beans in the steamer; cover and steam for 5 minutes until they are a brighter green and crisp-tender, then transfer the basket to the sink to rinse the beans under cool running water to stop the cooking process. Drain.
- ▶ Whisk together the walnut butter, tamari, toasted sesame oil, mirin, and sugar in a small bowl until well incorporated.
- ▶ Heat the oil in a wok or large skillet over medium-high heat. Once the oil shimmers, add the beans in batches; stir-fry for 30 seconds each, transferring them to a platter as you work.
- ▶ Add the garlic, ginger, and crushed red pepper flakes to the wok or skillet; stir-fry for 10 seconds, return all the beans; stir-fry for 30 seconds, and add the walnut butter mixture. Stir-fry until well coated, about 30 seconds. Taste and add crushed red pepper flakes, if desired. Serve hot.

Note: To make walnut butter, combine 2 cups roasted, unsalted walnut halves, 1/4 teaspoon kosher salt, and 2 teaspoons walnut or vegetable oil in a food processor; puree until smooth. The yield is 1 cup.

An earlier version of this recipe did not specify when to add the mirin, which gets whisked into the walnut butter sauce mixture; it also mistakenly did not include 1 teaspoon finely chopped ginger in the ingredients list.

Nutritions:

- ▶ *Calories: 123 kcal*
- ▶ *Carbohydrates: 14g*
- ▶ *Protein: 4g*
- ▶ *Fat: 7g*
- ▶ *Saturated Fat: 3g*
- ▶ *Sodium: 519mg*
- ▶ *Potassium: 395mg*
- ▶ *Fiber: 5g*
- ▶ *Sugar: 7g*
- ▶ *Vitamin C: 21mg*
- ▶ *Calcium: 79mg*
- ▶ *Iron: 2mg*

Frozen Berry Shakes

Frozen berries are a thrifty way of creating a healthy smoothie - pad it out with oats to make it extra filling. A delicious mixed berry smoothie is just seconds away when you blend up these ingredients. Use frozen fruit for a frosty treat at any time. It's hard to top the classic fruity tartness of a mixed berry smoothie! This beautifully pink smoothie is a breeze to make, and it's packed full of wonderful flavor and nourishing antioxidants.

This mixed berry smoothie is infinitely adaptable because you get to choose what frozen berries make up your smoothie! Craft your perfect combination of strawberries, raspberries, blueberries, and blackberries—or take a shortcut and used mixed frozen berries from the frozen fruit section of your supermarket.

Prep time: 5 minutes Servings: 2 servings

Ingredients:

- ▶ 1 cup blueberry (100 g)
- ▶ 1 cup strawberry (150 g), sliced
- ▶ ½ cup blackberry (75 g)
- ▶ ½ cup raspberry (65 g)
- ▶ 1 ½ cups non dairy milk (350 mL), of choice
- ▶ 1 cup Vegan greek yogurt (285 g)

Directions:

- ▶ Put fruit in a freezer bag. Seal and store in the freezer for up to 8-12 months.
- ▶ When ready to use, put non dairy milk, Vegan Greek yogurt, and frozen fruit into a blender and mix until the consistency is smooth.
- ▶ Enjoy!

Nutritions:

- ▶ *Calories: 291 kcal*
- ▶ *Carbohydrates: 50g*
- ▶ *Protein: 9g*
- ▶ *Fat: 7g*
- ▶ *Saturated Fat: 1g*
- ▶ *Sodium: 148mg*
- ▶ *Potassium: 594mg*
- ▶ *Fiber: 7g*
- ▶ *Sugar: 23g*
- ▶ *Vitamin C: 68mg*
- ▶ *Calcium: 338mg*
- ▶ *Iron: 2.5mg*

Tomato Pumpkin Soup

A bowl of Roasted Tomato Pumpkin Soup will keep you warm and full during these chilly fall and winter months. Fresh Roma tomatoes are roasted and pureed with pumpkin, shallots and garlic, and a few spices. Drizzle with a little olive oil and coconut cream and top with fresh basil.

Prep time: 10 minutes Servings: 2 servings

Ingredients:

- ▶ 6 large roma tomatoes (about 1-1/2 pounds total weight)
- ▶ olive oil
- ▶ kosher salt
- ▶ 1 large shallot (about 1/2 cup)
- ▶ 2 cloves garlic
- ▶ 1 teaspoon minced thyme
- ▶ 1 teaspoon smoked paprika

- ▶ 1/4 to 1/2 teaspoon of ground cinnamon (more or less to taste)
- ▶ 3/4 teaspoon sugar
- ▶ 1/4 teaspoon ground sage (or 1/2 teaspoon minced fresh sage)
- ▶ 1/4 teaspoon of freshly grated nutmeg
- ▶ 1/8 to 1/4 teaspoon cayenne pepper
- ▶ 1 tablespoon lemon juice
- ▶ 1-1/2 cups pumpkin puree (or 1 can store-bought)
- ▶ 4 to 5 cups homemade vegetable broth or [good quality store-bought]
- ▶ kosher salt, to taste (about 1 to 2 teaspoons)

To serve:

- ▶ coconut creamolive oil
- ▶ fresh basil leaves
- ▶ freshly ground black pepper

Directions:

- ▶ Preheat your oven to 375°.
- ▶ Wash and cut the tomatoes in half horizontally. Place the tomato halves, cut-side facing up onto a metal rimmed baking sheet. Drizzle with olive oil and season with a teaspoon of kosher salt.
- ▶ Roast the tomatoes on the middle rack of your preheated oven for 50 to 60 minutes. Let cool before transferring the tomatoes into your blender.
- ▶ Meanwhile, heat a large dutch oven on medium heat, sauté shallot in a teaspoon of olive oil until soft and translucent. Add in the minced garlic and cook for 1 minute.
- ▶ To the blender with the tomatoes, add the shallots and garlic, pumpkin puree, paprika, cinnamon, sugar, sage, nutmeg, and lemon juice. Puree until smooth.

▶ Add the tomato/pumpkin puree back into the dutch oven and stir in the vegetable broth (add more broth for a thinner soup). Taste, adding more salt as desired. Bring to a bubble and heat until piping hot.

▶ Ladle hot soup into bowls and serve with a drizzle of coconut cream and olive oil. Top with pepitas, fresh basil, and freshly ground black pepper.

▶ If using fresh sage, add it with the thyme to the sautéed shallot and garlic.

Nutritions:

▶ *Calories: 182 kcal*

▶ *Carbohydrates: 37g*

▶ *Protein: 6g*

▶ *Fat: 4g*

▶ *Saturated Fat: 0.6g*

▶ *Sodium: 2375mg*

▶ *Potassium: 1587mg*

▶ *Fiber: 9g*

▶ *Sugar: 22g*

▶ *Vitamin C: 83mg*

▶ *Calcium: 90mg*

▶ *Iron: 2.5mg*

Motivational Tips On Preserving the Food and Reusing the Food

If you want to add cheese to your spaghetti, cashew cheese is a great cheese substitute, and it has a long shelf life, about 10 days in the fridge. Just mix cashews, water, salt, and lemon juice, add parsley or chives in a food processor.

CHAPTER 20

DAY 17

On-Time With Avos And Salsa

Avos might have ancient Mexican roots, but they're as in demand today the world over as they were there thousands of years ago, probably because it's just so easy to add an avo...to everything! Whatever gets your sombrero in a spin, add an avo to it – really, anytime is guacamole time!

Vegan Zoodles

In this easy and fresh vegan dinner, zucchini noodles, or "zoodles," are a gluten-free, low-calorie substitute for traditional pasta. For best results, toss the zucchini pasta with the basil pesto sauce and serve right away.

Prep time: 30 minutes Servings: 4 servings

Ingredients:

- 5-6 medium zucchini (2 1/4-2 1/2 pounds total), trimmed
- ¾ teaspoon salt, divided
- 1 cup packed fresh basil leaves
- 2 cloves garlic, crushed and peeled
- ⅓ cup unsalted cashews
- 2-3 tablespoons lemon juice
- 2 teaspoons nutritional yeast
- ½ teaspoon ground pepper
- 1/4 cup plus 1 tablespoon extra-virgin olive oil, divided
- 1 cup grape tomatoes, halved

Directions:

- Using a spiral vegetable slicer or a vegetable peeler, cut zucchini lengthwise into long, thin strands or strips. If using a vegetable slicer, stop when you reach the seeds in the middle (seeds make the noodles fall apart). Place the zucchini "noodles" in a colander and toss with 1/4 teaspoon salt. Let drain for 10 to 15 minutes, then gently squeeze to remove excess water.
- Meanwhile, combine basil, garlic, cashews, lemon juice, Nutritions: al yeast, the remaining 1/2 teaspoon salt and pepper in a food processor. Pulse until coarsely chopped, scraping down the sides as needed. With the motor running, add 1/4 cup oil and continue to process until well combined. Set aside.

▶ Heat the remaining 1 tablespoon oil in a large skillet over medium-high heat. Add the drained zucchini noodles and gently toss until hot, 2 to 3 minutes. Transfer to a large bowl. Add the pesto and tomatoes. Toss gently to combine.

Nutritions:

▶ *Calories: 333kcal*
▶ *Carbohydrates: 17g*
▶ *Protein: 7g*
▶ *Fat: 29g*
▶ *Saturated Fat: 5g*
▶ *Sodium: 610mg*
▶ *Potassium: 893mg*
▶ *Fiber: 4g*
▶ *Sugar: 9g*
▶ *Vitamin C: 53mg*
▶ *Calcium: 71mg*
▶ Iron: 3mg

Spinach and Coconut Milk

This recipe is so amazing... It's Yummy, for starters. It's easy. It's cheap. It's accommodating for any style of eating; vegans, vegetarians, and allergy diets, just by switching up your fats—a very versatile dish.

Prep time: 10 minutes Servings: 4 servings

Ingredients:

- ▶ 3 tablespoons vegan butter
- ▶ 20 ounces flat-leaf spinach, washed and drained
- ▶ 2 shallots, halved and sliced
- ▶ 1 tablespoon minced fresh ginger
- ▶ 2 teaspoons minced jalapeno chile
- ▶ 2 tablespoons unbleached all-purpose flour
- ▶ 1/2 teaspoon ground cumin

- Pinch of sugar
- 1 cup coconut milk
- Kosher salt and freshly ground pepper

Directions:

- Heat scant 1 tablespoon vegan butter in a large Dutch oven over medium. Add spinach and cook, stirring, until just wilted, 3 to 5 minutes. Drain spinach in a sieve, pressing to remove excess liquid. Let cool slightly, then roughly chop.
- Return pan to medium heat and melt the remaining 2 tablespoons vegan butter . Add shallots, ginger, and jalapeno and cook until softened, 3 to 5 minutes. Stir in flour, cumin, and sugar, cook for 1 minute, then slowly whisk in coconut milk. Bring to a boil, reduce to a simmer, and cook until thickened, 1 to 2 minutes.
- Stir chopped spinach into coconut mixture and season with salt and pepper.

Nutritions:

- *Calories: 248 kcal*
- *Carbohydrates: 14g*
- *Protein: 7g*
- *Fat: 21g*
- *Saturated Fat: 16g*
- *Sodium: 165mg*
- *Potassium: 1009mg*
- *Fiber: 5g*
- *Sugar: 3g*
- *Vitamin C: 43mg*
- *Calcium: 165mg*
- *Iron: 6mg*

Fennel and
Green Beans Pesto Salad

This Green Bean & Roasted Fennel Salad is a light and fresh salad that is so simple yet incredibly flavourful. Blanched green beans and caramelized roasted fennel are tossed in a herb and caper sauce and topped with flaked almonds. This works just as well as a salad in summer as it does as a side dish in fall and winter, and it can be made up to 3 days in advance. It's Vegan, Paleo, Keto, and Whole30 too!

This salad is so simple and requires only a few ingredients, but it is full of flavor and absolutely delicious.

Prep time: 10 minutes Servings: 4 servings

Ingredients:

▶ 8 ounces green beans, trimmed

▶ 8 ounces orzo (1 1/4 cups)

▶ 2/3 cup (packed) chopped fresh dill

- ► 1/4 cup olive oil
- ► 2 tablespoons white balsamic vinegar
- ► 1 tablespoon fresh lemon juice
- ► 2 cups 1/3-inch cubes unpeeled English hothouse cucumber (about 8 ounces)
- ► 3/4 cup diced fresh fennel bulb

Directions:

- ► Cook green beans in a large saucepan of boiling salted water until just tender, about 5 minutes. Using a slotted spoon, transfer beans to plate. Add orzo to the same boiling water. Cook until tender, stirring occasionally; drain.
- ► Blend dill, oil, vinegar, and lemon juice in a mini-processor until almost smooth. Season dressing with salt and pepper.
- ► Cut beans crosswise into 1/2-inch pieces. Place in a large bowl. Add orzo, cucumber, and fennel; mix in the dressing. Season salad to taste with salt and pepper.

Nutritions:

- ► *Calories: 241kcal*
- ► *Carbohydrates: 24g*
- ► *Protein: 5g*
- ► *Fat: 14g*
- ► *Saturated Fat: 2g*
- ► *Sodium: 15mg*
- ► *Potassium: 310mg*
- ► *Fiber: 3.5g*
- ► *Sugar: 4g*
- ► *Vitamin C: 13mg*
- ► *Calcium: 45mg*
- ► *Iron: 1mg*

Grilled Avocado with Broccoli and Tofu

Charred broccoli and tofu-grilled avocados are a filling vegan main. A lightly sweet and bright lemon curry sauce lifts all of the flavors.

Prep time: 15 minutes Servings: 6 servings

Ingredients:

Charred broccoli, tofu + avocados

- ▶ 1/4 cup olive oil + extra
- ▶ 1 tbsp dijon or grainy mustard
- ▶ 1 clove of garlic, peeled + sliced (optional!)
- ▶ 2 tbsp chopped chives + blossoms if you've got them
- ▶ big pinch of chili flakes
- ▶ 5-6 sprigs of thyme, leaves roughly chopped
- ▶ 2 tbsp lemon juice + zest
- ▶ salt + pepper to taste

- ▶ ground cumin to taste
- ▶ 1 package of extra-firm tofu, cut into 1/2 inch slices
- ▶ 2 stalks of broccoli, stems removed
- ▶ 3 firms, but ripe avocados
- ▶ 1-2 barely ripe apricots

Sweet curry lemon sauce:

- ▶ 2 tbsp lemon juice
- ▶ 1 strip of lemon zest
- ▶ 1/2 tbsp dijon OR grainy mustard
- ▶ 1-2 tbsp maple syrup OR agave nectar
- ▶ 1/4 cup diced red onion
- ▶ fat pinch of mild curry powder
- ▶ small pinch of ground cumin
- ▶ splash of filtered water (more or less depending on desired consistency)
- ▶ salt + pepper
- ▶ 1/2 tsp tamari soy sauce
- ▶ 3 tbsp-1/4 cup olive oil

Directions:

- ▶ In a small bowl, whisk together the olive oil, mustard, garlic, chives, chili flakes, thyme, lemon juice, lemon zest, salt, pepper, and cumin. Set aside.
- ▶ Lay the tofu slices in a large dish and cut the broccoli into florets. Add the broccoli to the dish with the tofu slices. Pour the marinade mix over the tofu and broccoli. Cover and refrigerate, allowing to marinate for at least 1/2 an hour.
- ▶ While the tofu and broccoli are marinating, make the sweet lemon curry sauce. Combine the lemon juice, lemon zest, mustard, maple syrup, red onion, curry powder, cumin powder, water, salt, pepper,

tamari, and oil in a blender and blend on high until you have a completely smooth mixture. Check the sauce for seasoning and place it in the fridge while you grill.

▶ Preheat your grill to high. Cut the avocados in half, and remove all pits. Brush the exposed surfaces with oil and season with salt + pepper. Set aside.

▶ Start laying the tofu and broccoli on the grill. Cook until char marks appear on all surfaces, carefully flipping pieces of tofu and broccoli over here and there for even cooking. Remove all tofu and broccoli once it's sufficiently cooked/charred. Place avocado halves on the grill and cook until char marks appear. Remove and place on a serving platter.

▶ Chop up the tofu and broccoli into small pieces and toss them together in a medium bowl. Dice up the apricots and add them to the bowl as well. Toss with some more chopped chives or chive flowers if you want, and serve with the grilled avocado halves. Finish with drizzles of the sweet lemon curry sauce.

Nutritions:

▶ *Calories: 409kcal*
▶ *Carbohydrates: 18g*
▶ *Protein: 11g*
▶ *Fat: 36g*
▶ *Saturated Fat: 5g*
▶ *Sodium: 290mg*
▶ *Potassium: 707mg*
▶ *Fiber: 9g*
▶ *Sugar: 5g*
▶ *Vitamin C: 19mg*
▶ *Calcium: 407mg*
▶ *Iron: 2.6mg*

Motivational Tips On Preserving the Food and Reusing the Food

If you are craving some dessert like ice cream. Blend frozen bananas with a splash of almond milk in your food processor. This is like the texture of soft-serve ice cream, and the flavor is awesome with no added sugar!

CHAPTER 21

Load Up With Beans And Greens

Loaded with nutrient-dense vegetables, this beans and greens recipe is almost addicting. The sauce is light and flavorful, while the veggies offer a ton of healthy vitamins our bodies crave. Perfect any night of the week, this easy beans and greens recipe will keep you satisfied and coming back for more.

Sausage-Style Breakfast Patties

Nothing gives you better satisfaction than knowing you made your own breakfast rounds. It's quick and easy, the mixture can be made in advance, and the cooked patties can be thrown in the freezer and then microwaved for a quick minute. This recipe easily doubles. You can enjoy it right away, make it ahead of time for weekday breakfasts, or freeze it for later use. If you are sensitive to heat, feel free to reduce the amount of crushed red pepper or eliminate it altogether.

Prep time: 15 minutes Servings: 10 servings

Ingredients:

- 1 pound ground impossible vegan burger "meat"
- 1 teaspoon rubbed sage
- 1 teaspoon salt
- 1 teaspoon crushed red pepper
- ½ teaspoon ground marjoram
- ½ teaspoon ground black pepper
- ½ teaspoon onion powder
- ¼ teaspoon dried thyme leaves
- 1 tablespoon olive oil

Directions:

- Combine ground impossible vegan meat , sage, salt, crushed red pepper, marjoram, black pepper, onion powder, and thyme leaves in a large bowl; mix until evenly combined. Form mixture into 10 small patties.
- Heat oil in a large skillet over medium-high heat. Working in batches, cook patties for 3 minutes. Flip and cook 3 minutes more or until juices run clear. An instant-read thermometer inserted into the center should read at least 160 degrees F (73 degrees C). Transfer patties to a paper towel-lined plate to absorb any excess grease.

Nutritions:

- ► *per 1 patty: Calories: 110kcal*
- ► *Carbohydrates: 4g*
- ► *Protein: 8g*
- ► *Fat: 7g*
- ► *Saturated Fat: 2g*
- ► *Sodium: 171mg*
- ► *Potassium: 245mg*
- ► *Fiber: 1g*
- ► *Sugar: 0.4g*
- ► *Vitamin C: 5mg*
- ► *Calcium: 30mg*
- ► *Iron: 9mg*

Cabbage Rolls

These delicious traditional stuffed Cabbage Rolls are made with impossible vegan meat instead of ground sausage and ground beef with a sweet and tangy tomato sauce.

Prep Time: 35 minutes Servings: 12 rolls

Ingredients:

- ► 1 tablespoon olive oil
- ► 1/2 medium onion finely chopped
- ► 2 cloves garlic minced
- ► 1 can (15 ounces) tomato sauce
- ► 1 can (14.5 ounces) petite diced tomatoes
- ► 1 tablespoon cider vinegar
- ► 1 1/2 tablespoons brown sugar

Cabbage rolls:

- ▶ 1 large head green cabbage
- ▶ 1 lb ground impossible vegan meat
- ▶ 1/2 medium onion finely chopped
- ▶ 2 cloves garlic minced
- ▶ 3/4 cup Minute Rice (or parboiled rice)
- ▶ 1 tablespoon dried parsley
- ▶ 1/2 teaspoon paprika

Directions:

- ▶ Bring a large stockpot of water to boil. Add the whole head of cabbage and boil for 5 minutes. Remove to a colander to drain and cool. Once cooled, cut 1/2 inch off the stem end of the cabbage. Carefully remove 12 leaves and cut the tough rib out of the stem end in the shape of a V.
- ▶ In a large skillet, heat olive oil over medium heat.
- ▶ Add the onion and cook for 2-3 minutes, stirring several times. Reduce heat to low and add garlic—Cook for 1 minute, stirring constantly. Add the tomato sauce, diced tomatoes, cider vinegar, and brown sugar. Simmer for 10 minutes.
- ▶ Spoon a thin layer of tomato sauce in a 9 x 13-inch casserole dish. Mix the ground impossible vegan meat, onion, garlic, , rice, parsley, and paprika in a large bowl. Place about 1/3 cup of the "meat" mixture in the center of the cabbage roll. Bring in the sides and roll tight. Place tomato sauce in casserole dish. Repeat until all the cabbage rolls are made and in the casserole dish. Top with remaining tomato sauce.
- ▶ Cover with aluminum foil. Bake in a preheated 350-degree oven for 80-90 minutes

Nutritions:

- *per 1 roll: Calories: 192kcal*
- *Carbohydrates: 25g*
- *Protein: 10g*
- *Fat: 6.5g*
- *Saturated Fat: 3g*
- *Sodium: 218mg*
- *Potassium: 687mg*
- *Fiber: 5g*
- *Sugar: 8g*
- *Vitamin C: 61mg*
- *Calcium: 67mg*
- *Iron: 2mg*

Chai Protein Smoothie

Since we know convenience is a huge factor in today's day and age; this smoothie can be made the night ahead for a quick grab-and-go in the morning. The vanilla chai flavor comes from the plant-based protein itself, but feel free to add vanilla almond milk or vanilla protein mixed with some chilled chai tea. The combination of hearty spices with the flavor of the plant-based protein powder and the rest of the ingredients makes this smoothie recipe an incredible symphony of flavors.

This hearty and simple high-protein recipe smoothie is both delicious and incredibly healthy. Add the easiness and convenience factor, and you got yourself a new favorite recipe.

Prep time: 5 minutes Servings: 2 servings

Ingredients:

▶ 1 banana ideally frozen, for texture

- ► 2 cups spinach
- ► 1 scoop vanilla chai plant-based protein (Momentus is a great brand)
- ► ½ cup soy milk, plain
- ► ½ cup of water
- ► 1 tablespoon Spirulina
- ► ½ teaspoon maple
- ► ½ teaspoon cinnamon powder
- ► 2 teaspoons Almond Butter

Directions:

- ► Combine all ingredients in a blender. Blend and add extra milk if needed.
- ► Transfer to a mason jar, protein shaker bottle, or glass of choice. Top with fresh berries if desired and enjoy!

Nutritions:

- ► *Calories: 182kcal*
- ► *Carbohydrates: 25g*
- ► *Protein: 15g*
- ► *Fat: 5g*
- ► *Saturated Fat: 0.6g*
- ► *Sodium: 236mg*
- ► *Potassium: 627mg*
- ► *Fiber: 4g*
- ► *Sugar: 12g*
- ► *Vitamin C: 14mg*
- ► *Calcium: 171mg*
- ► *Iron: 4mg*

Spinach with Coconut

Prep time: 15 minutes Servings: 4 servings

Ingredients:

Spinach in Coconut Milk

- ► 1 lb frozen spinach, thawed
- ► ½ medium onion, finely diced
- ► 3 cloves garlic, crushed
- ► 1/2 tsp crushed ginger
- ► ½ tsp allspice
- ► ½ scotch bonnet pepper, seeds removed
- ► 1 ½ cup coconut milk
- ► ½ tsp sugar
- ► 1 tsp salt
- ► 1 tbsp canola oil

Directions:

▶ In a large skillet, heat canola oil, add the onion and garlic and sauté for couple of minutes. Add thawed spinach and ginger.

▶ In a separate bowl stir together coconut milk with sugar, salt and all spice.

▶ Pour the prepared coconut mixture over the sautéed spinach and continue cooking for next 10 minutes over medium high heat, stirring occasionally. Serve with diced tempeh if desired.

Nutritions:

▶ *Calories: 277kcal*
▶ *Carbohydrates: 13g*
▶ *Protein: 6g*
▶ *Fat: 25g*
▶ *Saturated Fat: 19g*
▶ *Sodium: 686mg*
▶ *Potassium: 920mg*
▶ *Fiber: 5g*
▶ *Sugar: 5g*
▶ *Vitamin C: 50mg*
▶ *Calcium: 137mg*
▶ Iron: 5mg

Motivational Tips On Preserving the Food and Reusing the Food

Some people feel like when they become vegan, they need to also simultaneously become zero-waste, minimalists, gluten-free, sugar-free, oil-free, fitness warriors, not to mention an expert in vegan

Nutritions: But why all the pressure? You're going to learn more and more about veganism with time. You can start to adopt these other lifestyle practices down the road if they even resonate with you at all.

CHAPTER 22

DAY 19

Dance With Asparagus And Spinach

When asparagus season is here, at last, you've got to make the most of it. Asparagus gets a beautiful char while roasting in the oven. Toasty around the edges and soft in the middle.

They add satiety and keep you full longer. Plus, when chickpeas roast in the oven and get crisp around the edges, it feels so satisfying to bite into them. It's finished with spinach, garlic, onions, and a squeeze of lemon.

Almond Chia Breakfast Pudding

If you haven't made chia seed pudding before, you might wonder how a couple of simple ingredients can turn into a thick dessert like this in the world. That's the beauty of chia seeds. If you've put them in smoothies or baked goods before, you've probably noticed that they get somewhat gelatinous after sitting in liquid for more than a few minutes.

While sometimes gross and snot-like in a smoothie, that property makes them perfect for this almond chia seed pudding because you don't need to add any other thickening agent, just chia, liquid, and flavoring.

Healthy almond chia pudding is an easy, naturally vegan, and gluten-free make-ahead breakfast or dessert that takes under 5 minutes to prepare!

Prep time: 5 minutes Servings: 2 servings

Ingredients:

- ► 1 1/2 cups unsweetened almond milk (or other milk types of choice)
- ► 1/4 cup chia seeds
- ► 1 Tbsp. agave syrup

- 1/2 tsp. almond extract
- 1 Tbsp. toasted slivered or sliced almonds
- 1/4 cup sliced fruit, optional (apple)

Directions:

- Combine all ingredients except toasted almonds and fruit and stir to mix well.
- Chill for at least two hours, preferably overnight. Stir 2-3 times throughout this time to disperse chia seed clumps.
- Divide between two dishes and top with almonds and fruit before serving. Will keep in the refrigerator for up to four days.

Notes

- To quick toast almonds, place in the microwave for about 1 minute.

Nutritions:

- *Calories: 235kcal*
- *Carbohydrates: 29g*
- *Protein: 5g*
- *Fat: 11g*
- *Saturated Fat: 1g*
- *Sodium: 117mg*
- *Potassium: 243mg*
- *Fiber: 8.5g*
- *Sugar: 19g*
- *Vitamin C: 2mg*
- *Calcium: 475mg*
- *Iron: 2mg*

Curry Cauliflower Rice

Have you tried cauliflower rice? Curry Cauliflower Rice is the perfect rice substitution that is low carb, very nutritious, and delicious. Cauliflower is processed with a food processor, sauteed with onion, garlic, ginger, bell pepper, and spices, and cooked in coconut sauce.

Curry cauliflower rice is ready and on the table in under 15 minutes! This vegan, whole30, ketogenic, and Paleo side dish recipe is so easy to make by using frozen cauliflower rice and a few go-to Indian spices.

Prep time: 10 minutes Servings: 4 servings

Ingredients:

- ▶ 2-3 cups cauliflower, about one head- medium sized
- ▶ 1 tablespoon coconut oil
- ▶ 1 small onion, finely chopped
- ▶ 3 cloves garlic, minced

- ▶ 1 teaspoon grated ginger
- ▶ 2 teaspoon turmeric powder
- ▶ 1 teaspoon cumin
- ▶ 1 teaspoon coriander
- ▶ 1/4 medium red bell pepper, diced
- ▶ 1 medium carrot, peeled and cut into strips
- ▶ 1/2 cup coconut milk
- ▶ 3/4 teaspoon salt, or to taste
- ▶ 1/4 teaspoon Cayenne pepper
- ▶ 1 green onion, chopped

Directions:

- ▶ To make cauliflower rice, grate cauliflower using a box grater or cut cauliflower into florets and process using a food processor. If using a food processor, a process in small batches. Set aside in a large bowl.
- ▶ Heat oil in a large saucepan or skillet on medium-high heat. Add onion, garlic, ginger, and cook until onion is soft, about 3 minutes.
- ▶ Add turmeric, cumin, coriander, and cook until fragrant. Stir in the bell pepper and carrots, cook stirring for a minute.
- ▶ Stir in the cauliflower rice to coat, add the coconut milk, and cover to cook for 8 minutes, occasionally stirring to prevent the cauliflower from sticking. Stir in spring onion, salt, and pepper to taste.

Nutritions:

- ▶ *Calories: 164kcal*
- ▶ *Carbohydrates: 15g*
- ▶ *Protein: 4g*
- ▶ *Fat: 11g*
- ▶ *Saturated Fat: 9g*
- ▶ *Sodium: 499mg*
- ▶ *Potassium: 680mg*

- *Fiber: 5g*
- *Sugar: 6g*
- *Vitamin C: 86mg*
- *Calcium: 63mg*
- Iron: 2.5mg

Italian Minestrone

Classic Italian minestrone soup is a colorful mix of vegetables, beans, fresh herbs, and ditalini pasta simmered in a savory tomato broth. Sauteing onions, celery, carrots, and squash delivers a flavor punch even before the soup begins to bubble on the stove. Pairing fresh ingredients with canned beans and tomatoes creates a quick stovetop dish.

Prep time: 10 minutes Servings: 6 servings

Ingredients:

- ► 1 tablespoon olive oil
- ► 1 cup yellow onion, ½-inch dice
- ► 1 cup celery, ½-inch dice
- ► 1 cup carrots, ½-inch dice
- ► 1 cup zucchini, ½-inch dice
- ► 1 cup yellow squash, ½-inch dice

- ▶ 1 tablespoon minced garlic
- ▶ 2 tablespoons tomato paste
- ▶ 28 ounces diced tomatoes, canned with juice
- ▶ 4 cups unsalted vegetable stock, plus more to thin out the soup
- ▶ 1 teaspoon kosher salt
- ▶ 2 sprigs of rosemary
- ▶ 1 bay leaf
- ▶ 1 teaspoon chopped oregano, or ½ teaspoon dried
- ▶ 15 ounces red kidney beans, rinsed and drained
- ▶ 1 cup green beans, trimmed and cut to ½-inch pieces
- ▶ black pepper, as needed for seasoning
- ▶ 1 cup dried pasta, Ditalini
- ▶ 2 teaspoons chopped parsley

Directions:

- ▶ Heat a large dutch oven or stockpot over medium-high heat and then add in oil.
- ▶ Once the oil is hot, add the onions, celery, and carrots, saute until lightly browned, 5 minutes.
- ▶ Add zucchini and yellow squash, saute for 2 minutes.
- ▶ Add garlic and saute for 30 seconds.
- ▶ Add tomato paste and saute for 30 seconds.
- ▶ Add diced tomatoes, vegetable stock, 1 teaspoon salt, rosemary, bay leaf, and oregano, stir to combine.
- ▶ Turn the heat to medium and bring the liquid to a vigorous simmer.
- ▶ Add red kidney beans and pasta to the pot, cook until pasta is al dente, about 10 minutes.
- ▶ Add green beans to the pot and cook until tender and bright green, about 3 minutes.
- ▶ Remove rosemary sprigs and add more vegetable broth as needed to thin out the soup, about 1 to 2 cups, warm before serving.

▶ Taste soup and season with more salt and pepper as desired.

▶ Garnish with parsley and serve hot.

Nutritions:

▶ *Calories: 257kcal*

▶ *Carbohydrates: 47g*

▶ *Protein: 12g*

▶ *Fat: 4g*

▶ *Saturated Fat: 1g*

▶ *Sodium: 1176mg*

▶ *Potassium: 905mg*

▶ *Fiber: 11g*

▶ *Sugar: 11g*

▶ *Vitamin C: 25mg*

▶ *Calcium: 130mg*

▶ *Iron: 4mg*

Avocado Mint Soup

Nutty flavored avocado is blended with fried onion, ginger & garlic to create a comforting soup.

Climate is cloudy these days, and we generally prefer to have hot piping soups for dinner. Avocado Mint soup is one such soup that has become a part of our regular dishes. Naturally, nutty-flavored avocado is blended with fried onion, ginger & garlic. The mix is then combined with olive oil, marinated crushed mint leaves, and cooked as a soup consistency. The soup is finally served with Whole wheat croutons.

Prep time: 5 minutes Servings: 2 servings

Ingredients:

- ▶ 2 Avocados
- ▶ 3 to 5 cloves Garlic, chopped
- ▶ 1 Ginger, chopped ~1 Tbsp
- ▶ 1 Onion, chopped

- 10 to 15 Mint Leaves (Pudina)
- Extra Virgin Olive Oil, 2 Tbsp or as required
- 2 Fresh Red chilies

Directions:

- To begin making the Avocado Mint Soup recipe, take a saucepan, add the required olive oil, and saute garlic, red chili, and onion. Allow it to cool.
- Blend avocado and the fried onion, garlic, and chili mix with ¾ cup of water in a blender.
- Pour the puree into the pan, add salt and the remaining water, and let it boil in low flame.
- Switch of the gas once you see the soup becoming frothy.
- Take a hand mortar, add 1 spoon of olive oil and mint leaves and grind it nicely. Add the mint mix into the soup.
- Soup is ready to be served. Serve Avocado Mint Soup along with Garlic Bread for a healthy and light dinner.

Nutritions:

- *Calories: 490kcal*
- *Carbohydrates: 28g*
- *Protein: 6g*
- *Fat: 43g*
- *Saturated Fat: 6g*
- *Sodium: 21mg*
- *Potassium: 1239mg*
- *Fiber: 15g*
- *Sugar: 6g*
- *Vitamin C: 135mg*
- *Calcium: 54mg*
- *Iron: 2mg*

Motivational Tips On Preserving the Food and Reusing the Food

Give yourself time. Everything we do is harder and requires more of our time in the beginning. So intentionally schedule some extra time when it comes to preparing meals; at least for the first few weeks, you'll get faster. Don't worry.

CHAPTER 23

DAY 20

Brain Boosting Day With Broccoli And Beans

The foods we eat can have a big impact on the structure and health of our brains. Eating a brain-boosting diet can support both short- and long-term brain function. The brain is an energy-intensive organ, using around 20 percent of the body's calories, so it needs plenty of good fuel to maintain concentration throughout the day.

Broccoli and other cruciferous vegetables are rich in fiber and nutrients. As well as being a low-calorie source of dietary fiber, broccoli and beans may be good for the brain. Broccoli is rich in compounds called glucosinolates. When the body breaks these down, they produce isothiocyanates. Isothiocyanates may reduce oxidative stress and lower the risk of neurodegenerative diseases.

Spinach and Greens Smoothie

A delicious way to add more veggies to your diet! This recipe is very versatile. You can change out the greens with whatever you want. Chia seeds give you added protein and energy. Hemp seeds will give you a boost of omegas!

Feel free to experiment with different flavors, and enjoy the pure energy that comes from eating delicious and good-for-you food!

Prep time: 10 minutes Servings: 2 servings

Ingredients:

► 2 cups fresh spinach
► 1 cup almond milk
► 1 tablespoon peanut butter
► 1 tablespoon chia seeds (Optional)

- 1 leaf kale
- 1 sliced frozen banana, medium sized

Directions:

- Blend spinach, almond milk, peanut butter, chia seeds, and kale together in a blender until smooth. Add banana and blend until smooth.

Nutritions:

- *Calories: 196kcal*
- *Carbohydrates: 28g*
- *Protein: 6g*
- *Fat: 8g*
- *Saturated Fat: 1g*
- *Sodium: 108mg*
- *Potassium: 584mg*
- *Fiber: 6g*
- *Sugar: 16g*
- *Vitamin C: 31mg*
- *Calcium: 331mg*
- *Iron: 2mg*

Turnip Carrot Salad

Turnips are inexpensive, easy to cook and store, and very nutritious. They are available almost all year round and are wonderful during the colder months of the year when not so many fruits and veggies are in season. Unfortunately, this vegetable is not very popular. You are not going to see many Instagram celebrities posting pictures of their turnip salad.

This is a simple little side dish that can be served as a switch from coleslaw. Turnips are usually mild and slightly sweet when they're small and have a nice firm crunch.

Prep time: 10 minutes Servings: 4 servings

Ingredients:

- ► 6 small purple-top turnips, peeled, ends trimmed
- ► 2 small carrots, peeled
- ► 1 large Granny Smith apple, peeled and cored
- ► 1 tablespoon freshly squeezed lemon juice
- ► 1 tablespoon onion, finely chopped
- ► 3 tablespoons vegetable oil
- ► 1 tablespoon apple cider vinegar
- ► 1-1/2 teaspoons sugar
- ► 1 tablespoon fresh parsley, chopped
- ► Salt and freshly ground black pepper to taste

Directions:

- ► Prepare the turnips, carrots, and apple using the shredding disk of a food processor or the largest holes on a box grater and combine in a large mixing bowl.
- ► Add the lemon juice and toss to coat. Add the onion, oil, vinegar, sugar, and parsley.

▶ Mix well. Season to taste with salt and freshly ground pepper. Cover and chill for one hour before serving.

Nutritions:

▶ *Calories: 161kcal*

▶ *Carbohydrates: 17g*

▶ *Protein: 1g*

▶ *Fat: 10g*

▶ *Saturated Fat: 1g*

▶ *Sodium: 118mg*

▶ *Potassium: 319mg*

▶ *Fiber: 3g*

▶ *Sugar: 12g*

▶ *Vitamin C: 26mg*

▶ *Calcium: 41mg*

▶ *Iron: 0.5mg*

Almond Macaroons

This recipe for almond macaroons is so simple and easy; you will want to make this your go-to recipe for every occasion! These almond macaroon cookies are quick and so delicious!

This recipe makes such awesome cookies in literally no time! These amazing almond macaroons are sweet, fragrant, crisp on the outside, and soft on the inside, the perfect cookie for a 5 o'clock tea or next to a cup of coffee.

Prep time: 15 minutes Servings: 20 cookies

Ingredients:

- ▶ 4 ounces almond paste (about 5 1/2 tablespoons
- ▶ 1/2 cup confectioners' sugar, plus more for dusting
- ▶ Pinch of coarse salt

- ► 1 full Tbsp of applesauce1/4 teaspoon pure vanilla extract
- ► 1/4 cup sliced almonds

Directions:

- ► Preheat oven to 300 degrees. Put almond paste, sugar, and salt in the bowl of an electric mixer fitted with the paddle attachment. Mix on medium speed until crumbly, about 3 minutes. Add applesauce and vanilla. Mix until smooth and thickened, about 3 minutes.
- ► Drop batter by tablespoons onto a baking sheet lined with parchment paper, spacing 2 inches apart. Place 2 almond slices on each mound of dough. Bake until cookies are golden brown, 20 to 25 minutes. Let cool completely on a wire rack. Just before serving, lightly dust cookies with sugar.

Nutritions:

- ► *per cookie: Calories: 43kcal*
- ► *Carbohydrates: 5.5g*
- ► *Protein: 1g*
- ► *Fat: 2g*
- ► *Saturated Fat: 1g*
- ► *Sodium: 8mg*
- ► *Potassium: 27mg*
- ► *Fiber: 0.5g*
- ► *Sugar: 5g*
- ► *Vitamin C: 0mg*
- ► *Calcium: 13mg*
- ► *Iron: 0.1mg*

Cream of Spinach Soup

Puréed vegetable soups can be lean and spare or rich and creamy, spicy or subtle, hot or cold. They can be vegetarian or quite meaty. And much of the cooking time is just for simmering. With a touch of nutmeg and some cream, this spinach soup is a classic combination, and its flavor justifies that distinction.

There's no better way to warm up a new year than with a bowl of this Cream of Spinach Soup! Creamy, rich, and so easy to make. Dinner will be ready in less than 20 minutes!

Prep time: 15 minutes Servings: 8 servings

Ingredients:

▶ 1 tablespoon olive oil

- 2 tablespoons vegan butter
- 1 large shallot, chopped
- 2 garlic cloves, minced
- 2 tablespoons flour
- 1 pound spinach leaves
- 2 1/2 cups coconut cream
- 2 cups vegetable broth
- Pinch of freshly grated nutmeg to taste
- 1/2 teaspoon cayenne pepper (optional)
- Salt and freshly ground pepper to taste
- 1/2 cup grated vegan parmesan cheese

Directions:

- In a large pot or dutch oven, heat the olive oil and vegan butter over medium heat until the butter has melted. Add the shallot and garlic and sauté until softened and fragrant.
- Add the flour and stir to combine, cooking for about a minute to get rid of the raw flour taste. Then, add the spinach and cook until wilted, about 5 minutes.
- Add the coconut cream, veggie broth, nutmeg, cayenne, salt, and pepper, and cook until thickened, about 5 minutes. Add the vegan parmesan and stir to combine. Taste for seasoning and adjust if necessary.
- If the soup is not thick enough, you can dissolve a bit more flour into some broth or coconut cream and add that mixture to the pot. Continue cooking until the soup is as thick as you>d like.
- Serve immediately.

Nutritions:

- *Calories: 342kcal*
- *Carbohydrates: 10g*

- ▶ *Protein: 6g*
- ▶ *Fat: 33g*
- ▶ *Saturated Fat: 24g*
- ▶ *Sodium: 275mg*
- ▶ *Potassium: 577mg*
- ▶ *Fiber: 3g*
- ▶ *Sugar: 1g*
- ▶ *Vitamin C: 18.5mg*
- ▶ *Calcium: 117mg*
- ▶ *Iron: 3mg*

Motivational Tips On Preserving the Food and Reusing the Food

Get Stocked. The lifestyle change is going to be complicated if you've got nothing on hand to work with. So start by stocking up on the pantry essentials. If you're just starting off, don't go to the extreme and forbid yourself from having any treat foods only to look at other people who have them and then envy them. Not veganism is just as fun.

CHAPTER 24

DAY 21

Cozy Day With Pudding, Tart, And Soup

Cuddling up in your cozy wear and having some recipes that would warm you up. Yes, it's that time of the year where you feel relaxed and sometimes lazy. But your soul is happy when you feed it some warm food.

Olives and Spinach Mini Quiche Cups

Serve these olives mini quiches as an appetizer or at your next brunch. They are so easy to make using refrigerated pie crusts.

Prep time: 15 minutes Servings: 9 quiche

Ingredients:

- ▶ 1 box (14.1 oz) refrigerated Keebler Ready Crust Graham Pie Crust (2 Count), softened as directed on box
- ▶ 1 tablespoon olive oil
- ▶ 3 cups chopped fresh spinach
- ▶ 3 tsp of egg replacer powder
- ▶ ½ cup coconut cream
- ▶ ½ cup shredded vegan cheese blend (2 oz)
- ▶ 1/8 teaspoon black pepper
- ▶ 3 tablespoons chopped green onions

Directions:

- ▶ Prevent your screen from going dark while you cook.
- ▶ Heat oven to 375°F. Spray 24 mini muffin cups with cooking spray. Remove 1 pie crust from pouch; place flat on work surface. With a 2 1/2-inch round cutter, cut 12 rounds. Press rounds in bottoms and up sides of 12 mini muffin cups. Repeat with the second pie crust.
- ▶ In a 10-inch skillet, heat olive oil over medium heat. Add spinach; cook and stir until wilted, about 5 minutes.
- ▶ In a medium bowl combine egg replacer powder with coconut cream, vegan cheese, pepper, green onions, and cooked spinach. Spoon about 1 tablespoonful mixture into each crust-lined cup.
- ▶ Bake 20 to 25 minutes or until puffed and crust edges are golden brown. Cool 5 minutes. With the tip of a knife, loosen and remove quiches from cups.

Nutritions:

▶ *Calories: 275kcal*

▶ *Carbohydrates: 28g*

▶ *Protein: 4g*

▶ *Fat: 17g*

▶ *Saturated Fat: 6g*

▶ *Sodium: 211mg*

▶ *Potassium: 130mg*

▶ *Fiber: 1g*

▶ *Sugar: 10g*

▶ *Vitamin C: 3.5mg*

▶ *Calcium: 59mg*

▶ *Iron: 1.6mg*

Mushroom Asparagus

These roasted vegetables are the perfect side dish with fried Tofu.

Prep time: 10 minutes Servings: 4 servings

Ingredients:

- ► 1 bunch fresh asparagus, trimmed (14 spears that typically measure 9-10 inches long and 1/2-3/4 inch thick)
- ► ½ pound fresh mushrooms, quartered
- ► 2 sprigs fresh rosemary, minced
- ► 2 teaspoons olive oil
- ► kosher salt to taste
- ► freshly ground black pepper to taste

Directions:

- ► Preheat oven to 450 degrees F (230 degrees C). Lightly spray a cookie sheet with vegetable cooking spray.

▶ Place the asparagus and mushrooms in a bowl. Drizzle with the olive oil, then season with rosemary, salt, and pepper; toss well. Lay the asparagus and mushrooms out on the prepared pan in an even layer. Roast in the preheated oven until the asparagus is tender, about 15 minutes.

Nutritions:

▶ *Calories: 47kcal*
▶ *Carbohydrates: 5g*
▶ *Protein: 3g*
▶ *Fat: 3g*
▶ *Saturated Fat: 0g*
▶ *Sodium: 43mg*
▶ *Potassium: 324mg*
▶ *Fiber: 2g*
▶ *Sugar: 2g*
▶ *Vitamin C: 5mg*
▶ *Calcium: 20mg*
▶ *Iron: 2mg*

Cabbage Slaw

▶ *This coleslaw is quick and easy to make. It is even easy to make in advance. This coleslaw recipe is packed with fresh*

lively flavors that wake up anything you serve it with. Try this as a topping to sandwiches. You won't believe how easy coleslaw is to make at home.

Prep time: 15 minutes Servings: 4 servings

Ingredients:

▶ 1 medium cabbage (about 2 pounds), outer leaves removed

▶ 3 medium carrots, peeled and shredded

▶ 1/2 cup loosely packed fresh parsley leaves, coarsely chopped

▶ 1 cup (170 grams) Vegan mayonnaise,

▶ 2 tablespoons apple cider vinegar or more to taste

▶ 2 tablespoons Dijon mustard or coarse ground mustard

- ▶ 1 teaspoon celery seeds
- ▶ 1/4 teaspoon fine sea salt or more to taste
- ▶ 1/4 teaspoon fresh ground black pepper or more to taste

Directions:

- ▶ Quarter the cabbage through the core and then cut out the core. Cut each quarter crosswise in half and finely shred. Place the shredded cabbage in a very large bowl (you will have 6 to 8 cups).
- ▶ Add the shredded carrot and parsley to the cabbage and toss to mix.
- ▶ In a separate bowl, stir the vegan mayonnaise, vinegar, mustard, celery seeds, salt, and pepper together. Taste for acidity and seasoning, then adjust as desired. Pour two-thirds of the dressing over the cabbage and carrot, then mix well.
- ▶ If the coleslaw seems dry, add a little more of the dressing. Eat right away or let it sit in the refrigerator for about an hour to let the flavors mingle and the cabbage to soften.

Nutritions:

- ▶ *Calories: 288kcal*
- ▶ *Carbohydrates: 23g*
- ▶ *Protein: 7.5g*
- ▶ *Fat: 20g*
- ▶ *Saturated Fat: 2g*
- ▶ *Sodium: 789mg*
- ▶ *Potassium: 764mg*
- ▶ *Fiber: 7g*
- ▶ *Sugar: 11g*
- ▶ *Vitamin C: 132mg*
- ▶ *Calcium: 167mg*
- ▶ *Iron: 3mg*

Eggplant and Zucchini Curry

Curry usually means a lot of time and effort to get that amazing yellowish cream that we all love eggplant, and zucchini curry may be the solution. It is easy, tasty, and has seasonal ingredients for a great result. If you are looking for a meatless option for a comforting curry, this eggplant and zucchini curry may be the solution. It is easy, tasty, and has seasonal ingredients for a great result.

A big plus of this recipe, besides how easy it is, is that it is quick to make, and you can take the curry base and add any type of veggie — bell peppers, onion, broccoli, broccolini, mushrooms, etc.

Prep time: 10 minutes Servings: 4 servings

Ingredients:

▶ 5 tablespoons olive oil or coconut oil

▶ 14 oz extra-firm tofu patted dry and cut into ¾ inch cubes

▶ 1 medium onion quartered and thinly sliced

▶ 2 tablespoons red curry paste

▶ 2 zucchini cut lengthwise and then into ½ inch pieces

- ▶ 1 large eggplant cut into ½ inch pieces
- ▶ 1 can (13.5 oz) full fat or light coconut milk
- ▶ ¼ c cilantro chopped
- ▶ ½ lime juiced
- ▶ salt

Directions:

- ▶ Heat 2 tablespoons of oil in a large non-stick pan. Add tofu and cook on medium heat until nice and brown on all sides, about 10 minutes. Transfer to a plate lined with a paper towel.
- ▶ Add the remaining 3 tablespoons of oil to a pan along with onion, zucchini, eggplant and cook on medium-high heat for 7-10 stirring occasionally until eggplant is brown and soft. (Add more oil if needed)
- ▶ Add curry paste and stir for 1 minute. Return tofu back into the pan, add coconut milk, and bring to a simmer. Season with salt, lime juice, remove from the heat, and add cilantro.
- ▶ Serve eggplant curry over steamed rice or pasta.

Nutritions:

- ▶ *Calories: 549kcal*
- ▶ *Carbohydrates: 23g*
- ▶ *Protein: 21g*
- ▶ *Fat: 47g*
- ▶ *Saturated Fat: 22g*
- ▶ *Sodium: 42mg*
- ▶ *Potassium: 955mg*
- ▶ *Fiber: 10g*
- ▶ *Sugar: 7g*
- ▶ *Calcium: 747mg*
- ▶ *Iron: 7mg*

Motivational Tips On Preserving the Food and Reusing the Food

Consider adding, not taking away. This is not a deprivation diet. It's an eat-in abundance lifestyle, so a lot of times when people first think about veganism, they start to think about all the things that they can't have, like beef, chicken, fish, cheese, yogurt, butter, ice cream, or milk. But that's not the right mindset; instead, what we want to do is to focus on all of the things we are adding and let these foods naturally replace the other stuff adding more plant-based dairy alternatives like soy, almond, rice, or coconut milk and yogurts. More whole grains, fruits, and more vegetables.

CHAPTER 25

DAY 22

Flexible With Grains And Tomatoes

Whole grains are known for being healthy, hearty, and flavorful. But if you cook them with a little less water and a little more seasoning, grains become addictive all on their own.

Macaroni and Cheese

A very quick and easy fix to a tasty side dish. Fancy, designer mac and cheese often cost forty or fifty dollars to prepare when you have so many exotic and expensive cheeses, but they aren't always the best tasting. This recipe is cheap and tasty.

Prep time: 10 minutes Servings: 4 servings

Ingredients:

- 1 (8 ounces) box elbow macaroni
- ¼ cup vegan butter
- ¼ cup all-purpose flour
- ½ teaspoon salt
- ground black pepper to taste
- 2 cups non dairy milk
- 2 cups shredded Vegan Cheddar cheese

Directions:

- Bring a large pot of lightly salted water to a boil. Cook elbow macaroni in the boiling water, occasionally stirring until cooked through but firm to the bite, 8 minutes. Drain.
- Melt vegan butter in a saucepan over medium heat; stir in flour, salt, and pepper until smooth, about 5 minutes. Slowly pour non dairy milk into butter-flour mixture while continuously stirring until mixture is smooth and bubbling, about 5 minutes. Add vegan Cheddar cheese to the "milk" mixture and stir until cheese is melted 2 to 4 minutes.
- Fold the macaroni into cheese sauce until coated.

Nutritions:

- *Calories: 611kcal*

- ▶ *Carbohydrates: 58g*
- ▶ *Protein: 28g*
- ▶ *Fat: 30g*
- ▶ *Saturated Fat: 5g*
- ▶ *Sodium: 814mg*
- ▶ *Potassium: 466mg*
- ▶ *Fiber: 4g*
- ▶ *Sugar: 10g*
- ▶ *Vitamin C: 0mg*
- ▶ *Calcium: 566mg*
- ▶ *Iron: 2mg*

Tomato Eggplant Spinach Salad

Grilled eggplant and roasted tomatoes hold up well against sturdy spinach and add a smoky touch to this simple end-of-summer salad. Chef Justine lightly fries the chickpeas in oil to help infuse the flavors of the spices.

Prep time: 15 minutes Servings: 2 servings

Ingredients:

- ▶ 2 medium tomatoes
- ▶ 1 large eggplant
- ▶ 2 shallots
- ▶ 1 ½ cups chickpeas, canned
- ▶ 2 Tbsp of toasted almonds
- ▶ Few fresh mint leaves, chopped
- ▶ 1 tsp of Chickpea spice blend (cumin - garlic - paprika - sumac)
- ▶ 1 lemon

- ▶ 2 cups of Spinach
- ▶ 2 Tbsp of crumbled Vegan Feta cheese
- ▶ 3 Tbsp of olive oil

Directions:

Wash produce before use

Cook the tomatoes
- ▶ Heat the oven to 375°F.
- ▶ Core the tomatoes and cut them into thirds.
- ▶ Line a sheet pan with foil and spread the tomato slices on it in an even layer. Season with salt. Roast the tomatoes until completely soft and slightly charred, about 30 minutes.
- ▶ Meanwhile, prepare the eggplant.

Prep the eggplant, shallots, almonds
- ▶ Slice the eggplant into ½-inch thick rounds and generously season with salt. Set on a paper towel to drain.
- ▶ Peel and thinly slice the shallots.
- ▶ Chop the almonds.
- ▶ Rinse the chickpeas.
- ▶ Pick the mint leaves off the stem and chop the leaves.

Grill the eggplant
- ▶ In a 12-inch frying pan over medium-high heat, warm 2 tablespoons oil until hot but not smoking. Rinse the eggplant and pat dry. Grill the eggplant in batches, if necessary, until soft in the middle and charred, about 4 minutes on each side. Remove from the frying pan and set aside to cool. Don't clean the pan.

Cook the chickpeas
- ▶ In the same pan used to cook the eggplant, warm 1 tablespoons oil over medium heat until hot but not smoking. Add the shallots, season with salt, and cook until beginning to soften about 1 minute. Add the

chickpeas, and the spice blend, season with salt and cook until the chickpeas are heated for about 2 minutes.

Make the dressing

► Zest and juice the lemon.

In a small bowl, combine the lemon zest and juice with 2 tablespoons of oil. Season with salt and pepper.

Serve

Cut the eggplant into bite-sized pieces. Toss the spinach with the grilled eggplant, roasted tomatoes, chickpeas, and mint in a salad bowl. Drizzle with the dressing. Top with the almonds and vegan feta cheese and divide evenly between two plates.

TIP: To evenly salt the eggplant, line a plate with paper towels and sprinkle the paper towels generously with salt. Line with the eggplant slices and sprinkle salt on top.

Nutritions:

► *Calories: 595kcal*
► *Carbohydrates: 46g*
► *Protein: 16g*
► *Fat: 42g*
► *Saturated Fat: 6g*
► *Sodium: 382mg*
► *Potassium: 1471mg*
► *Fiber: 18g*
► *Sugar: 19g*
► *Vitamin C: 42mg*
► *Calcium: 239mg*
► *Iron: 5mg*

Cauliflower Hummus

Cauliflower hummus is a delicious chickpea-free version of hummus that's low-carb, keto, paleo, and Whole30 friendly. It's creamy, savory, veggie-packed, and you'll love it just as much as my authentic hummus recipe.

Prep time: 10 minutes Servings: 12 servings

Ingredients:

- ▶ 4 cups Cauliflower florets (~1 lb)
- ▶ 1/4 cup Extra virgin olive oil (divided)
- ▶ 1/2 cup Tahini
- ▶ 2 cloves Garlic (minced or just chopped into a few pieces)
- ▶ 2 tbsp Lemon juice
- ▶ 1 tsp Sea salt
- ▶ 1 1/2 tsp Cumin

- ▶ 1/4 tsp Paprika
- ▶ 3-5 tbsp Water

Directions:

- ▶ Preheat the oven to 400 degrees F. Grease a nonstick baking sheet.
- ▶ Toss cauliflower with 2 tbsp olive oil. Spread in a single layer on the baking sheet so that every floret touches the pan.
- ▶ Roast the cauliflower in the oven for about 35-45 minutes, until browned and falling-apart soft.
- ▶ Pour the lemon juice, 2 tablespoons of water, and the remaining 2 tablespoons olive oil into a powerful blender or food processor. Add the roasted cauliflower, tahini, garlic, sea salt, cumin, and paprika. Puree until very smooth, stopping to scrape down the sides occasionally.
- ▶ If it's too thick, thin out with 1-3 more tablespoons of water, 1 tablespoon at a time. (I used 4 tablespoons total, 2 in the previous step and 2 to thin out more.)

Nutritions:

- ▶ *Calories: 112kcal*
- ▶ *Carbohydrates: 5g*
- ▶ *Protein: 3g*
- ▶ *Fat: 10g*
- ▶ *Saturated Fat: 1g*
- ▶ *Sodium: 217mg*
- ▶ *Potassium: 171mg*
- ▶ *Fiber: 2g*
- ▶ *Sugar: 1g*
- ▶ *Vitamin C: 22mg*
- ▶ *Calcium: 55mg*
- ▶ *Iron: 1.5mg*

Grilled Tofu, Broccoli, and Pineapples

Take your tofu talents to tropical locales with this rice and vegetable stunner guaranteed to part the clouds and let in the sunshine. Teriyaki and pineapple combine for a delightful sauce, coating the crispy tofu with bright flavors. But not just tofu; the rice, broccoli, and red bell pepper sop up the sauce, making the entire meal feel like you've just soaked up the sun.

Prep time: 10 minutes Servings: 4 servings

Ingredients:

- ▶ 1/2 cup crushed pineapple with juice or 3/4 cup pineapple chunks in juice
- ▶ 1/2 cup water
- ▶ 2 tablespoons lime juice
- ▶ 1/4 cup maple syrup

- ► 2 cloves garlic
- ► 2 tsp. soy sauce
- ► 1 tbsp. white miso
- ► 1 tsp. ginger paste
- ► 1 tsp. sesame oil
- ► 1 pound extra-firm tofu, lightly pressed to remove water and cut into 8 slices
- ► 1/2 medium onion, cut into thin wedges
- ► 1 bunch broccoli, cut into florets, and lightly steamed~ 1 cup
- ► sliced green onions and black sesame seeds for garnish
- ► rice to serve ~ 2 cups of brown cooked rice, divided

Directions:

- ► Preheat the oven to 375. Lay the tofu in an oiled baking dish, sprinkle the onion over it, and pour the prepared sauce on top. Cover and bake for 25 minutes. Remove the cover and add the pineapple chunks, and bake uncovered for 10 more minutes. (If you want, you can turn the broiler on to brown the pineapple slightly for part of this time.)
- ► Serve by placing the tofu and broccoli over a bed of rice and spooning sauce and pineapple pieces overall. Sprinkle with sliced green onions and sesame seeds.

Nutritions:

- ► *Calories: 320kcal*
- ► *Carbohydrates: 47g*
- ► *Protein: 15g*
- ► *Fat: 10g*
- ► *Saturated Fat: 1g*
- ► *Sodium: 220mg*
- ► *Potassium: 347mg*
- ► *Fiber: 3g*

- *Sugar: 19g*
- *Vitamin C: 10mg*
- *Calcium: 254mg*
- *Iron: 3mg*

Motivational Tips On Preserving the Food and Reusing the Food

If you're new to vegan, take advantage of the different mock meats, also known as textured vegetable proteins, that are available at most large chain grocery shops. This helps in your transition for sure, and if you don't know how to cook tofu available in most meat shops, as well as with the time you start to substitute for more wholesome plant-based sources.

CHAPTER 26

Questions And Answers About Vegan Meals, Vegan Diets, Etc

A healthy vegan diet has many health benefits, including lower rates of obesity, heart disease, high blood pressure, high blood cholesterol, type 2 diabetes, and certain types of cancer. It may take planning to get enough protein, iron, zinc, calcium, vitamins D and B12, and omega-3 fats from foods or supplements. A healthy vegan diet can meet all your nutrient needs at any stage of life, including when you are pregnant, breastfeeding, or older adults.

Question 1: What do vegans eat?

Absolutely loads of stuff. There's a misconception that vegans only eat 'vegetables,' but the better way to think of it is that vegans eat plants. Once you do that, you realize that this means potatoes, rice, pasta, bread, lentils, chickpeas, beans, soy, grains, seeds, nuts, fruits, oils, and vegetables, among others.

These days it's also easy to find and create convincing substitutes for many animal products, so you don't have to worry about missing out on anything if you're new to veganism or thinking about giving it a try. There's a way to veganism everything from sausages and burgers to steak, chicken, and cheese.

Question 2: Do I need to be a good cook to go vegan?

Absolutely not. Going vegan is easier than ever before, with microwave meals and frozen food that you can throw in the oven. Not to mention the rapid increase in plant-based options available in restaurants, cafes, takeaways, and fast-food chains.

But cooking is something that's worth getting good at. You'll save money, have far more control over what you consume, and be healthier as a result. It really is one of life's most valuable skills.

Question 3: Is a vegan diet expensive?

Like any diet, it's as expensive as you want it to be. But veganism is definitely suited to the cash-strapped among us.

Staples such as grains (rice, bread, pasta, oats, quinoa) and legumes (beans, peas, chickpeas, lentils, soybeans) are not only extremely affordable but widely available. As for fruit and veg, these should be a part of everyone's diet – whether vegan or not – and so the cost is the same for anyone.

There's also been an explosion of plant-based products on the market in recent years, making it easier than ever to enjoy the things you did as an omnivore without breaking the bank.

Question 4: Are there health issues that might spur from a vegan diet?

Diet-related health issues occur not because the diet is vegan but because it is inadequate. Both vegan and non-vegan diets can be inadequate.

An optimal vegan diet is health-protective. A whole foods plant-based diet is the only diet that has been clinically proven to reverse cardiovascular disease and even halt or reverse early stages of prostate and breast cancers.

Cardiovascular disease, diabetes, prostate, and breast cancers are in most cases created by inadequate Nutritions: and other unhealthy lifestyle factors. These easily preventable diseases affect and kill almost everyone in the developed world, yet only a tiny minority of the population is on a vegan diet.

Question 5: Is it easy to stay on a healthy vegan diet? Does it require extensive knowledge?

Once we have acquired the set of skills required to perform a task well, we do it with ease. When our taste preferences are trained to enjoy the plant-based foods that are optimal for our health, it only makes staying on a healthy vegan diet easier than not staying on it.

Designing and sticking with any healthy diet, not just a vegan one, requires focus, mindfulness, and learning about Nutritions: . The reward of better health outweighs the time and effort invested. Knowledge and application of nutritional science are vital for everyone to lead a healthy life.

Question 6: Is replacing meat with a vegan burger justified considering that a vegan burger may contain highly processed ingredients and may have been transported long distances?

Eating a vegan burger does not perpetuate animal exploitation. Eating animal products does.

There are places that sell supposedly "higher welfare" animal products, but the reality is that the most "humanely" produced animal products involve treatment that would, were humans involved, constitute torture.

All animal products involve injustice, torture, and killing. We would never send our companion animals whom we treat as family members to a slaughterhouse. The animals we have not bonded with personally are any different from the ones we have.

All animal products, including those from locally raised animals, are far more environmentally taxing than plant-based foods flown across the globe.

It is a myth that a vegan diet must include expensive artificial substitutes for animal products. The truth is that processed foods designed in a laboratory such as mock meats and fake cheese, although vegan, cannot be part of any healthy diet.

Question 7: Are animal products so unhealthy that it doesn't matter what we eat instead once we eliminate them?

We know that salt, white sugar, white flour, all types of oils, isolated proteins, artificial sweeteners, petroleum-derived additives, alcohol, and fried foods could be just as, if not more harmful to our health than animal products are. It is also common knowledge that most of us need to significantly increase our intake of health-promoting foods, particularly raw vegetables loaded with thousands of beneficial discovered and undiscovered micronutrients.

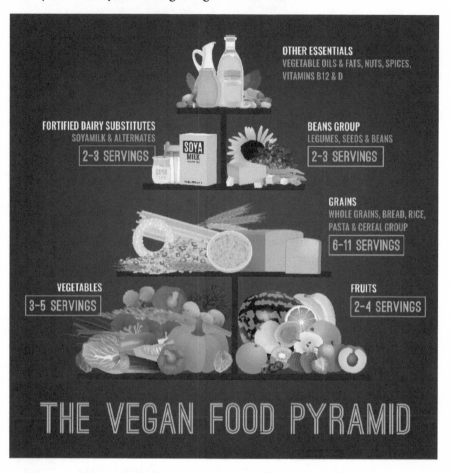

THE VEGAN FOOD PYRAMID

Only consuming as little as below 5% of our calories derived from animal products have no detrimental health consequences. Consuming 10–15% of our calories from animal products is the range where some of us get sick, and some of us don't. When consuming above 30% of calories derived from animal products, everyone gets sick.

Question 8: Where do vegans get their protein from?

We seem to have developed a modern obsession with protein, and people often assume that a diet without meat equals a diet lacking in protein. But this couldn't be further from the truth, as protein is found in all plants.

You heard that right. It really is in everything from beans, lentils, nuts, and soya to spinach, broccoli, peas, and grains. Not only are these sources of protein versatile and delicious – they're good for you, other animals, and the planet.

CONCLUSION

Both vegetarians and vegans choose not to eat meat and fish. However, veganism is a stricter form of vegetarianism that prohibits the consumption or use of any products that come from animals, including dairy, eggs, honey, leather goods, wool, and silk. Vegetarians may eat dairy products, eggs, honey, and other byproducts that do not involve the slaughter of animals. However, there are several variations of the vegetarian diet. For example, some vegetarians choose to eat eggs but not dairy products. Vegan diets generally include a range of fruits, vegetables, nuts, seeds, grains, pulses, and "meat substitutes" that derive from these food types.

Both vegetarian and vegan diets may provide health benefits, including reduced body weight, lower cholesterol levels, and decreased risk of cardiovascular disease. However, it is important for vegans to ensure that they are meeting all of their Nutritions: al requirements. For example, plants do not naturally contain vitamin B-12, so vegans and may need to consume fortified foods or take dietary supplements to get enough vitamin B-12.

FINAL WORDS

Helping the Reader Help Themselves

I f I cook you a nice vegan meal, you will be fed for a day. If I show you how to cook a nice vegan meal, you, dear reader, can feed yourself forever. Unleash your inner chef and discover tons of delicious vegan recipe ideas. This list is sure to make even the most passionate meat-eater change their mind about vegan food.

The collection of vegan recipes in this cookbook is perfect for all occasions. Whether you are looking for the perfect dish to impress someone special, or just need some inspiration to keep your meals interesting, this cookbook can help you with that!

Each recipe is written by a talented chef and comes with a photo of the finished product. We love to make vegan food look as tasty as possible. Therefore, you'll find plenty of mouth-watering photos of the dishes. Plus, we've added nutritional information, preparation time, and cooking time for each recipe. You now have all the information you need to begin a successful vegan diet. While, at first, you may experience some adverse side effects, they will go away if you stick with the vegan diet. It may seem harsh, but it's worth it. You will notice the results!

Finally, thank you for making it through to the end of this book. I hope it is informative and has provided you with all the tools you need to achieve your goals, whatever they may be.

Disclaimer: Nutritional information for each recipe was obtained from the *Verywell Fit* nutrition calculator.[1]

1 https://www.verywellfit.com/recipe-nutrition-analyzer-4157076

COOKING AND MENTAL
HEALTH REFERENCES

Those of us who are middle-aged remember our moms telling us that millions of kids go to bed hungry at night. That was true then, but unfortunately, it is still true today, even in the wealthiest countries. I started this cookbook series because I believed that we could eat healthy and cheap meals at home that were friendly to the planet and the animal kingdom. What I did not anticipate in 2018 and 2019 was how my focus would change. It is important to now talk about something that is taboo in most polite conversations. People are still embarrassed to talk about this — like this is something that is an individual fault and not a societal issue. However, as you can see from the references I have gathered here, this is now a societal crisis. We need to address this, and I resolved in the past two years that I would add a few pages in each of my cookbooks to bring this into the discussion table.

Let's talk about emotional hunger. Yes, there are many kinds of hunger, and this kind is no longer a remote topic that just a few individuals must face on their own. As the current US surgeon-general has indicated in his groundbreaking book (referenced below), loneliness and social withdrawal are plaguing the US and wealthy countries. I have added a few references here that may help you begin to wrap your head around how big this issue is in modern society. Let me be clear: home cooking is not some magic bullet that will magically remove your feelings of loneliness. Please understand that broader societal changes are at play, and there are no magic bullets that individuals can invoke to alleviate the distress easily or quickly. However, home cooking can play a role in combating feelings of loneliness and in building your own tribe or community. This is a societal issue with massively powerful trends behind them, and we are kidding ourselves that there is one magical or easy cure. However, every tiny bit helps.

It is not an accident that all societies until recently have relied on communal feasts to foster a sense of community. It is not an accident that every military force makes such elaborate rituals of meals. Wait! Even high-tech companies like to make extravagant free meals available to their workers to get them to stay indoors and exchange ideas. Think about it: why don't these high-tech companies ask their workers to eat their meals in their cubicles? Wouldn't that improve productivity? What do these immensely powerful corporations know about fostering a productive work environment and getting the most out of their workers that the common person on the street does not?

It is my hope that this cookbook series gets you thinking about this topic. Reach out to your family and friends. They are suffering from this silent crisis just as much as you. If there is one good thing that can come out of the trauma of the past two years with this global pandemic, it is this: we can no longer pretend that things are all ok and shut up and carry on. No, we can acknowledge the problems and reach out for help and find solutions. I sincerely hope that the references herein will be useful to you on your journey. Peace out!

Online References:

1. https://www.google.com/search?q=cooking+and+mental+health
2. https://www.bing.com/search?q=cooking+and+mental+health

3. https://www.southernliving.com/healthy-living/mind-body/cooking-therapy-mental-health

4. https://www.ecu.edu.au/newsroom/articles/research/chefs-kiss-research-shows-healthy-home-cooking-equals-a-healthy-mind

5. https://www.wsj.com/articles/a-road-to-mental-health-through-the-kitchen-1418059204

6. https://www.livekindly.com/7-surprising-ways-cooking-can-boost-your-mental-health/

7. https://medium.com/the-shadow/dealing-with-anxiety-with-the-help-of-cooking-44a267c3f9e7

8. https://www.verywellhealth.com/cooking-class-mental-health-5223665

9. https://emeraldpsychiatry.com/3-mental-health-benefits-from-cooking-at-home/

10. https://www.verywellmind.com/mental-health-benefits-of-cooking-your-own-food-5248624

11. https://www.nytimes.com/2022/10/09/opinion/burnout-friends-isolation.html

12. https://www.youtube.com/watch?v=_aSLhz00U7s

Other References

1. https://www.mentalhealth.org.uk/sites/default/files/Feeding-Minds.pdf

2. Farmer, et al. (2018) Psychosocial Benefits of Cooking Interventions: A Systematic Review. Health Educ. Behav. Doi: 10.1177/1090198117736352

3. Firth et al., (2020) Food and mood: how do diet and nutrition affect mental wellbeing? BMJ.

4. Hutchinson, J. et al. (2016) Evaluation of the effectiveness of the Ministry of Food cooking programme on self-reported food consumption and confidence with cooking. Public Health Nutrition. Doi:10.1017/S1368980016001476

5. https://www.scientificamerican.com/article/food-for-thought-was-cooking-a-pivotal-step-in-human-evolution/

6. Nickrand, H. L., & Brock, C. M. (2017). Culinary grief therapy: Cooking for One Series. *Journal of Palliative Medicine, 20*(2), 181–183. doi: 10.1089/jpm.2016.0123

LEAD NUTRITIONAL ADVISOR (USA)

Christine VanDoren is a certified personal trainer and nutritionist with a business degree from Missouri State University. Her passion is helping others learn how strong and healthy they can become by transforming their daily habits. Christine spends most of her time in the gym and learning how she can influence others through positivity!

Christine's Blog is: https://edgeoflongevity.com/

LEAD NUTRIOTIONAL
ADVISOR (EUROPE)

My name is Tanja Milenkovski MPH RD LD. I was born in Serbia, and as a kid I liked to cook with my mum, so this passion stayed, till today. I finished Medical school for a Dietitian Nutritionist and I have a Master's degree in Public Health from Medical University of Belgrade. For me food "isn't just something that I need to eat so I could function", in one way it represents my lifestyle and how I see the world. If you are healthy on the inside and satisfied with how you look, you will feel good and be happy, so this is my philosophy in life. I have many years of experience in the field of nutrition and I helped many people through the years with their nutrition and other health problems. Some people have to change their eating habits because of health, some because of intolerance for specific ingredients, and many people just want to eat healthier and be healthier overall. As a dietitian nutritionist I started to work in 2004. in one of the preschools in Belgrade, Serbia. I'm in charge of planning meals for more than 4,700 children, of whom we currently have 132 children with various allergies such as allergies to milk, gluten, diabetes, and children with special needs (Down's syndrome, autism, ADHD....). I have also worked in a Youth Center for the past 6 years, helping young moms get their body and health back, and also stay healthy during the pregnancy. During all my years as a nutritionist I have worked with many clients with a variety of needs and desires, so there probably isn't a thing I haven't heard of or worked with.

Nutrition is something that has always intrigued and interested me. And now I am here and upfront with you. I'm here to be honest, and with a great desire, help and raise awareness about the importance of nutrition and how easy and enjoyable it can be to make it and keep it actually healthy. Don't wait for a diagnosis to scare you before you decide to change your life habits. It doesn't matter how small the change is, it is important that it is permanent! A good nutritionist will save us time, money, nerves and most importantly health. When I say time, I mean losing it in a sea of information through net. Money, because it will save us from throwing money at unnecessary supplements, diets and ingredients. And above all, it will make us healthier.

ABOUT
JORDAN RILEY

Jordan Riley came into veganism slowly at first. She always loved animals, but she did not see the contradiction between loving animals and eating animal products at first. She does not know how it happened, but she slowly evolved into veganism. She also did not see the connection between increasing mental illness in this society and our culture of fast food and eating out by ourselves. However, a few trips abroad convinced her that the emotional richness of daily life in these countries overseas was connected in some intangible way to their culture being so focused on home-cooked meals and dining in with family. For some time now, Jordan has wondered if most of these cookbook authors are focusing on the wrong benefits of their cookbooks. Surely, cookbooks must promote home cooking and the benefits of cooking at home, and meals shared with near and dear ones.

Jordan is extraordinarily happy to record the great mental health and loneliness discussions with Trisha. This cookbook is so much better because of the additional pages I was able to add to the book on these important topics.

Also, Jordan is grateful for the great advice she received from Christine and Tanja. This cookbook is so much better because of the nutritional advice that they were able to provide.

Jordan can be reached at authorjordan@veganeasyquick.com

Her website is https://www.veganeasyquick.com

TRISHA HOUGHTON
(MENTAL HEALTH ADVISOR)

My name is Trisha Houghton, and I am a mental health professional who has worked in crisis management, individual, and group counseling throughout the past 15 years. I cannot speak enough on the importance of mental health. In 2022, we still have such a mixed relationship with mental health in a time where we urgently need to treat it as importantly as we do our physical health. We cannot have one affected without the other. I am currently a holistic life coach and certified autoimmune holistic nutrition specialist. From physical, mental, emotional, familial, and career issues to coaching through issues of imposter syndrome, burnout, lack of self-esteem, self-sabotage and my personal favorite; stress management, I absolutely love my job and those I work with to feel better mental and physically! Find more about myself and my services at www.houghtonlifecoaching.com

CONNECTED AROUND THE TABLE

By Trisha Houghton

I f you are a human with a heartbeat, the likelihood of you feeling lonely at some point is quite high. If you are a minority, a marginalized group or sect, a young adult, an older adult, or have a disability or a mental health condition, you are most probably going to experience loneliness.

We are currently facing an uphill battle, especially in this post-pandemic era, that we currently live.

We all need to feel connected...to have contact with other humans and live our lives in communities. Even if you are a self-proclaimed "home-body," chances are you still want people to be around whom you can choose to interact with or not.

The freedom of choice...It's a funny thing because I think at our core, we all want to just simply know we could if we wanted to ... be that we could go out to eat, could have a social gathering, could throw a party. We all just want to be able to choose.

If only something happened in recent history that reinforced this concept and showed us, we do, indeed need one another...Something that reinforced the innate need for community, friendship, and simply just sharing space with another human being... Oh, that's right, it did!

The pandemic taught us more than I think we even realize, and its effects continue to be discovered. At the center of the pandemic, it reminded most of us that life is uncertain, mortality is real, and the world has many aspects that are simply unpredictable.

It taught us the value of health, of time, and honestly led us to self-evaluations; The reexamining of our collective and individual "why. "..Why do we work hard...why do we have family...why do we hang out with those we do...why do we spend our time as we do...why do we fight for a certain cause or choose to do anything at all...why do we spend time and energy on some things and not others? And then the question of what...what do we want? What do we need? What can we do...and then, how can we do it, and most importantly, who can we do it with...

The pandemic taught us that isolation is directly associated with mental health conditions and feelings of loneliness. That loneliness again doesn't discriminate and it is not just something the elderly are the most likely group to experience.

The pandemic shone a light on how much our mental health is highly influenced by the people we surround ourselves with.

Not being able to go to work, go out to eat, or even make dinner for our extended family, being unable to go to the gym, movie theater, or even the store really connected the dots as to how much we undervalued simply being able to be in the same room as another, never mind going out in public!

Many kids had both parents home for meals, as family members became everything; teachers, friends, peers, and the end all and be all of social interaction. It is my thought and hope that family meals and time spent cooking together have become invaluable time spent.

Cooking also became a hobby for many. This is our hope in this book; to reinforce togetherness. Food has been something sought after whilst in the company of others since the beginning of time. Gathering around the table with food; it's communal and unites us. Around the table has been the host of so many life-changing moments such as first dates and other major life decisions. It has also been the setting for debating topics, discussing shared interests, and sharing life stories. All these moments have happened around the table, usually while sharing a meal.

For many, the pandemic highlighted the vitally important topic of our universal need for connectedness; of being together. Whether "together" means living with someone, or simply going into public to have people around you in the same space, it highlighted that the option; the mere choice to see, interact, gather and live life with people including families, groups, strangers and friends, is something we have taken advantage of.

While there are many negatives from the pandemic, I think the focus on our why, which it nearly demanded we all do, is invaluable. And I think this is also how we can honor all the lives cut short by the pandemic, living with intention. Many have realized their "why" or their "what" isn't what they want their life to be anymore. Switching careers is at an all-time high as we are collectively compelled to change whatever the pandemic made us realize. From seeking increased overall life satisfaction to ending relationships whether friendships or partnerships; many have now chosen to go a different path. Friend groups are chosen more wisely as is how we spend our time and whom we spend it with.

People, in general, are living more and waiting less…one day is less heard and emphasis on the moment is highlighted.

The pricy gift it gave us remains as we ask questions that evaluate our "why" and choose our "who." We all value time spent just a little more and feel gratitude for being in company, together.

However, 2 years is a long time, and we are seeing the mental and physical toll loneliness has taken.

History of Together:

Babies are 100% reliant on others; their survival depends on it. Harvard (2020) data shows that "we are heavily shaped by our social environment and experience significant distress when our social ties are threatened or broken."

Brain studies show that adverse life events such as being shunned by a community, being excluded, and feeling isolated activates the same areas in the brain that respond to physical pain (Harvard, 2020).

Loneliness can cause the development of mental health conditions and oppositely, loneliness may be in response to mental health conditions.

While studying social engagement and mental health, it was found that loneliness is correlated with mental health in a self-perpetuating cycle (Harvard, 2020). What does this mean? It means that symptoms of mental health conditions often cause one to isolate however, that isolation worsens those mental health conditions.

Physical and Mental Health Affects:

Loneliness and mental health as studied by the Mental Health Foundation found:

- Almost 50% of people feel left out or alone

- Relational deficiencies can be linked with increased risk of heart disease or stroke

- Loneliness changes the structure and processes with the brain

- 27% of Americans rarely or never feel that there are people who understand them

- Loneliness causes autonomic, endocrine, and immune functioning problems as well as the development of various health conditions that can take time before surfacing

- Loneliness reduces one's resilience, particularly in the elderly population

- Loneliness also gives 50% increased risk of developing dementia

Loneliness literally effects the heart. In fact, patients diagnosed with heart failure have a nearly 4x increased risk of death, a 68% increased risk of hospitalization, and 57% increased risk of emergency department visits (National Academies of Sciences, Engineering, and Medicine, 2020).

Those with few to no social relationships (characterized by social isolation or loneliness) have a 29 % increased risk of experiencing an incident from coronary heart disease and a 32% increased risk of stroke.

Social isolation is associated with increased risk of premature mortality across all causes.

This is by no means an exhaustive list of how loneliness can affect one's physical and mental health. I like how the Mental Health Foundation explained it; "when the needs: of security, to feel validated, to be affirmed, and to feel significant within a relationship, to be accepted by a stable, dependable, and protective other person, to have an impact on another person, to express love...when these needs go unmet, the result is loneliness who's ripple effects are sadly, limitless.

Which Groups are Affected:

Every person is affected by loneliness to varying degrees.

However, there are certain groups more likely to experience feelings of loneliness. These groups include but are not limited to, marginalized individual/groups including the LGBTQIA+ community, the elderly, those with mental health or physical health conditions, and young adults!

In many of these groups, these individuals have a largely increased chance of social isolation, to some extent. And social isolation is a precursor to loneliness.

The National Academies of Sciences, Engineering, and Medicine (2020) defines social isolation as "the objective state of having few social relationships or infrequent social contact with others) and loneliness (a subjective feeling of being isolated)."

What we know and understand the longer we study life is that feelings of loneliness are not just growing, they are skyrocketing. Yet, they remain to be a global public health crisis that now affects all age groups (National Academies of Sciences, Engineering, and Medicine, 2020).

In fact, studies show that loneliness in the elderly can result in both dysfunction and distress and can even be diagnosed as a disease (National Academies of Sciences, Engineering, and Medicine, 2020).

Watch Out for Young Adults:

So, what do we do? What can we do? We can support more, criticize less. We can take ownership in our role to help mold our youth. We can pay attention to young adults and teens as the numbers for this group in experiencing loneliness are heavily increasing.

Whether it be because of COVID-19, too much social media time leading to compare more and feel less than, or less face to face interaction, the CDC (2022) reports 63% of young adults are suffering high rates of loneliness with symptoms of both anxiety and depression.

Why, when we know that the youth are our future world leaders, teachers, scientists, and innovators. Why do we not support this age group?

They are in the most challenging time of their life deciding everything from what they like, what they want their life's work to be, to how and who to love while learning and discovering how to be treated and how to treat others.

Instead of mostly criticizing them, how about we talk to them, even if it is texting them. How about we, as the adults, take the initiative and join them in their world of social media, games, or anything else they are interested in. They have literally their as well as our future ahead of them and yet they remain the most highly criticized population. Instead of sought after, young adults are too often, written off or kept at a distance.

As we have thoroughly discussed, we all need one another and young adults are in desperate need of our kindness, our knowledge, our acceptance, our time, and to be the focus of our attention, especially during this odd time of transition back to some sort of "normal life," post COVID.

We must give them a reason to get away from "behind the screen." We need give them our attention and show them support and love, not isolate them.

I am a firm believer in doing better when we know better. Now, you know so let's all, do better.

SOURCES:

https://mcc.gse.harvard.edu/reports/loneliness-in-america

IS LONELINESS MAKING MY MENTAL HEALTH STRUGGLES HARDER? | MENTAL HEALTH AMERICA (MHANATIONAL. ORG)

LONELINESS AND MENTAL HEALTH - MENTAL HEALTH FOUNDATION

National Academies of Sciences, Engineering, and Medicine. 2020. Social Isolation and Loneliness in Older Adults: Opportunities for the Health Care System. Washington, DC: The National Academies Press. https://doi.org/10.17226/25663.

Finally, Must-Reads on Loneliness and Self-Compassion

1) *Together: The Healing Power of Human Connection in a Sometimes Lonely World*

   By Dr. Vivek H. Murthy,19th Surgeon-General of the USA, https://www.amazon.com/dp/B07LFDNM9K

2) *Self-Compassion: The Proven Power of Being Kind to Yourself* by Kristin Neff (Associate Professor, UTexas, Austin)

   https://www.amazon.com/dp/B004JN1DBO

Your Comments Genuinely Help Others

A big thank you for trusting my book with your time, attention, and support. Here are three points to remember about reader comments (aka book reviews):

1. I read all reader comments so I can fix any errors and improve my book. As an author, I feel that my output is either *getting better every day or getting left behind* by the world. I believe that :
An author's persistence plus your genuine enthusiasm expressed in comments and purchases = good quality books.

2. I don't buy anything without checking the reviews. <u>Your reviews will help readers just like you, so thanks.</u>

3. Now, you're all ready to drop a comment, but analysis paralysis gets the better of you. You might think: *What would I even write about? Who's going to read/care about my review, anyway?*

Well, for starters, your reviews help the author. Also, we know that reviews play a big part in the decisions of readers. So, to help you snap out of your analysis paralysis, here are some questions on which other readers would want your opinions:

- What did you think of the recipes? What did you like or not like about any recipe?

- How quick and easy are these recipes? Any suggestions for the author on which ones are not quick and easy? Which ones are quick and easy?

- What did you think of the book cover and the general graphic design of the book?

Think of these questions as kick-starters for your review.

Please drop your honest opinions here:

https://www.amazon.com/review/create-review?ASIN=B0BWMKK2TR

Or click or scan the QR Code below:

That would make my day! Thank you!

Please download a free PDF with
a) all the recipes shown in this book, and
b) 50 bonus recipes from here:
https://BookHip.com/NJGBDLB

Or click or scan the QR code below:

Happy reading,

Jordan

P.S.: Thanks, www.kindlepreneur.com for the QR codes and www.
booklinker.com for the universal links.

JORDAN RILEY BOOKS

To download, scan the QR Code or click on the images above or the link below:

https://mybook.to/VEGANSINGLES

To download, scan this QR code or click on the images above or the link below:

https://mybook.to/VEGANFAMILIES

To download, scan this QR code or click on the images above or the link below:

https://mybook.to/VEGANLOWCARB

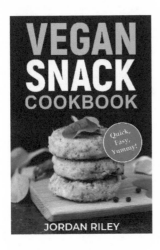 

To download, scan this QR code or click on the images above or the link below:

https://mybook.to/VEGANSNACKS

To download, scan this QR code or click on the images above or the link below:

Made in United States
Troutdale, OR
01/04/2024

16690929R00202